VOLUME 18

D1516381

MARK

Walter P. Weaver

ABINGDON PRESS
Nashville

MARK

Copyright © 1988 by Graded Press

All rights reserved.

This book is printed on recycled, acid-free paper.

Library of Congress Cataloging-in-Publication Data

Cokesbury basic Bible commentary.
  Basic Bible commentary / by Linda B. Hinton . . . [et.al.].
    p.   cm.
  Originally published: Cokesbury basic Bible commentary. Nashville: Graded Press, © 1988.
  ISBN 0-687-02620-2 (pbk. : v. 1 : alk. paper)
  1. Bible—Commentaries. I. Hinton, Linda B. II. Title.
[BS491.2.C65   1994]
220.7—dc20   94-10965
                                                                              CIP

ISBN 0-687-02637-7 (v. 18, Mark)
ISBN 0-687-02620-2 (v. 1, Genesis)
ISBN 0-687-02621-0 (v. 2, Exodus–Leviticus)
ISBN 0-687-02622-9 (v. 3, Numbers–Deuteronomy)
ISBN 0-687-02623-7 (v. 4, Joshua–Ruth)
ISBN 0-687-02624-5 (v. 5, 1–2 Samuel)
ISBN 0-687-02625-3 (v. 6, 1–2 Kings)
ISBN 0-687-02626-1 (v. 7, 1–2 Chronicles)
ISBN 0-687-02627-X (v. 8, Ezra–Esther)
ISBN 0-687-02628-8 (v. 9, Job)
ISBN 0-687-02629-6 (v. 10, Psalms)
ISBN 0-687-02630-X (v. 11, Proverbs–Song of Solomon)
ISBN 0-687-02631-8 (v. 12, Isaiah)
ISBN 0-687-02632-6 (v. 13, Jeremiah–Lamentations)
ISBN 0-687-02633-4 (v. 14, Ezekiel–Daniel)
ISBN 0-687-02634-2 (v. 15, Hosea–Jonah)
ISBN 0-687-02635-0 (v. 16, Micah–Malachi)
ISBN 0-687-02636-9 (v. 17, Matthew)
ISBN 0-687-02638-5 (v. 19, Luke)
ISBN 0-687-02639-3 (v. 20, John)
ISBN 0-687-02640-7 (v. 21, Acts)
ISBN 0-687-02642-3 (v. 22, Romans)
ISBN 0-687-02643-1 (v. 23, 1–2 Corinthians)
ISBN 0-687-02644-X (v. 24, Galatians–Ephesians)
ISBN 0-687-02645-8 (v. 25, Philippians–2 Thessalonians)
ISBN 0-687-02646-6 (v. 26, 1 Timothy–Philemon)
ISBN 0-687-02647-4 (v. 27, Hebrews)
ISBN 0-687-02648-2 (v. 28, James–Jude)
ISBN 0-687-02649-0 (v. 29, Revelation)
ISBN 0-687-02650-4 (complete set of 29 vols.)

02 03—10 9 8 7 6 5 4 3

MANUFACTURED IN THE UNITED STATES OF AMERICA

Contents

Outline of Mark

VI. Rejection and Miracles (6:1-56)
  A. Rejection of Jesus in his hometown (6:1-6)
  B. The mission of the disciples (6:7-13)
  C. The death of John the Baptist (6:14-29)
  D. The feeding of the five thousand (6:30-44)
  E. Jesus' walking on the sea (6:45-52)
  F. The crowds coming to Jesus (6:53-56)
VII. Christianity and Judaism (7:1-37)
  A. Ritual defilement; the Corban issue (7:1-23)
  B. The status of the non-Jew (7:24-30)
  C. Healing outside Galilee (7:31-37)
VIII. The Expectations of Discipleship (8:1–9:1)
  A. The feeding of the four thousand (8:1-10)
  B. Pharisaic questioning (8:11-13)
  C. The disciples' lack of understanding (8:14-21)
  D. The man healed in stages (8:22-26)
  E. The way of Jesus and his followers (8:27–9:1)
IX. The Transfiguration of Jesus (9:2-50)
  A. The transfiguration (9:2-8)
  B. The Elijah expectation (9:9-13)
  C. Jesus' exorcism (9:14-29)
  D. Second prediction of the Passion (9:30-32)
  E. Lessons on discipleship (9:33-37)
  F. Friends and enemies of Jesus (9:38-41)
  G. Admonitions to disciples (9:42-50)
X. From Galilee to Judea (10:1-52)
  A. Marriage and divorce (10:1-12)
  B. Receiving the Kingdom (10:13-16)
  C. The prior demand of the kingdom (10:17-22)
  D. The requirements of discipleship (10:23-31)
  E. The third prediction of the Passion (10:32-34)
  F. The disciples argue over greatness (10:35-45)
  G. The seeing blind Bartimaeus (10:46-52)
XI. Jesus Enters Jerusalem (11:1-33)
  A. Jesus' entrance into the city (11:1-11)
  B. Cursing the fig tree (11:12-14)
  C. The cleansing of the Temple (11:15-19)

Introduction to Mark

Authorship, Date, Place of Writing

We do not know who wrote the Gospel of Mark. According to Eusebius (fourth century), Papias, a bishop of the second century, reported the tradition that Mark was composed by (John) Mark based upon the recollections of Peter. It does not seem likely today that this tradition is reliable. Mark does not have the character of an eyewitness piece of work; it is, rather, based upon oral traditions circulating in the Markan church. The author must remain anonymous, though he must also be given credit for having created the Gospel as a type of literature, since Mark was the first to be written.

The customary date for Mark is around A.D. **70, at about the time of the Jewish revolt against Rome. Of course, no one really knows and the Gospel does not say, but internal indications point to a time when conditions were severe for some Christian communities. And Mark also seems to be aware of the destruction of the Temple in** A.D. 70 (see 13:2).

Rome is given in early sources (second century on) as the traditional site of writing, but again the Gospel itself does not say where it originated. Other places have been suggested, such as Syria, Egypt, or Asia Minor. We cannot know for sure, though a reasonable case can still be made for the Roman location. For example, the persecution of Christians at Rome under the lunatic emperor Nero in the sixties could be the source of certain problems reflected in Mark.

Purpose of the Gospel

Why the Gospel was written has to be inferred. Certainly Mark wished to set out the Gospel as he understood it. Beyond that, he likely meant to address the situation posed by hard times for the Christian community. Mark looks at his time apocalyptically. He sees that the suffering now inflicted on the Christians is not accidental, but points to the time of the end, when the faithful will experience tribulation.

Other related problems appear, such as false messiahs and false prophets in the church (13:6, 22), coming to terms with the destruction of the Jerusalem Temple (13:1-2), accomplishing the universal mission of the church (13:10), and enduring to the end (13:11-13).

We might further suppose that Mark—probably not consciously—was responding to the situation in the church when the tradition about Jesus was growing dramatically and probably getting out of bounds. What Mark did was to take a large slice of the oral Jesus tradition and commit it to writing. In this way he fixed its form forever and prevented any further development. In a sense Mark represents the initial effort towards the formation of a canon.

The Synoptic Problem

The first three Gospels are called "synoptic" gospels because of their broad similarity. Following a long period of debate, scholarship concluded that this similarity was not accidental, that Mark was written first and then used independently by both Matthew and Luke. In addition, Matthew and Luke had a second source, which we do not any longer possess, but from which they drew substantial material. This source is called "Q." It contains the non-Markan material common to Matthew and Luke.

So Mark was written first and served as a source for both Matthew and Luke. The author of Mark, then, even though anonymous, has greatly influenced Christian history and literature. He was certainly a creative figure and, as the church came to recognize, composed a work of inspiration.

Style and Sources

Mark's style of writing is very elementary, even rough. Though his Greek is correct, he writes in a popular fashion, in the way of oral storytelling. His language is not complex and he obviously did not intend to produce a work of high literary merit. Characteristic of his style is the coordinating sentence—lots of "and's" coupled with modest use of subordinating clauses.

There is also a sense of urgency; Mark likes the word *immediately* (NRSV) or *at once* (NIV), for example. Yet Mark's thought is also very subtle, and his theological intention is not always easy to grasp.

As to sources, it is not so apparent that Mark had any beyond the oral material that lay at hand in his community. There has been some success in identifying a collection of miracle stories, perhaps a collection of parables and of Scripture proof-texts. Certainly also the Passion narrative had attained some fixed form before Mark set pen to papyrus, but for the most part Mark had no models to emulate.

Themes in Mark

Mark 1:15, *The kingdom of God* is near, points to the major Markan theme. Mark takes up the message of Jesus and renews it for his own time and situation. The Kingdom in Mark is to be understood apocalyptically; the end approaches and brings with it struggle and hostility. The Markan community sees itself passing through the final hours of tribulation. Suffering is inevitable and must precede the time of the end.

At the same time the apocalyptic outlook carries certain implications for discipleship, another of Mark's major concerns. Through the portrayal of the historical disciples Mark implements his own view. The picture of the disciples is largely negative; they repeatedly fail to understand Jesus or even to remain loyal to him. In the end they abandon him to his fate in the world. One of them denies him; another betrays him.

This picture is so powerful in the Gospel that it cannot be accidental. Mark is evidently campaigning for his own view of discipleship—perhaps against others in his community—a view which insists that following Jesus, who was crucified, necessarily entails the possibility of suffering and sacrifice.

Other matters appear in the Gospel, though more indirectly. Mark's portrayal of Jesus discloses the Markan christology (concept of Christ). The twin titles of *Son of God* and *Son of man* are most characteristic for Mark. They combine with the picture of the suffering one to provide a view of Mark's paradoxical Christ.

It is also apparent from the internal evidence of the Gospel that Mark's community has separated from Judaism. It is probably a community which has its own roots in Judaism, but has become of mixed Gentile-Jewish-Christian character. Such issues as sabbath observance, ritual regulations, and the value of the law generally can be seen as having already been determined in the Markan community. These debates with Judaism are not so bitter as, say, in Matthew; in fact, it seems that they are already settled for Mark and his community. What we are hearing in the Gospel appear to be mostly the echoes of those controversies.

Mark also contains the silence-theme, better known as the "messianic secret." A feature of Mark is the repetition of commands by Jesus to those who have been healed to be silent, or, alternatively, to others (including demons) not to disclose Jesus' identity. This peculiarity of Mark has been long recognized to come basically from the author of the Gospel, but there has been no unanimity as to its meaning.

The silence commands are actually of three types: (1) commands to demons (1:25); (2) commands to be silent about healings (1:44-45; 5:43; 7:36-37; 8:26); and (3) commands to be silent about Jesus' identity (1:34; 3:11-12; 8:30). The first—the only clear example—is the oldest of all the types and perhaps even became the inspiration for the others. Originally these commands were simply part of the commanding word of the exorcist by which he gained control over the demons; they had nothing to do with Jesus' identity or with suppression of Jesus' reputation as a healer.

The second two show Mark's handiwork. Jesus urges those whom he has healed to say nothing—there is one exception in 5:19-20—though he is often unsuccessful. At the same time there are many healings in which no injunction to silence is given. Mark is probably trying to put some restraints on the picture of Jesus as a miracle worker. There is no doubt for Mark that Jesus does mighty deeds; yet at the same time there is much more to the story of Jesus. In particular, there is the message of the cross, which unveils the true meaning of Jesus. So it is the paradoxical portrayal of Jesus as the powerful yet suffering one which is underlying the peculiar mixture of silence and openness in Mark.

The identity sayings are similarly motivated. Jesus is pictured as not wishing it known who he is, except at the moment of his own self-disclosure (14:62). Caesarea Philippi is the key scene here (8:27-33). Jesus publicly disclaims any messianic titles until they are given the appropriate meaning—that is, until the suffering role becomes apparent.

PART ONE   Mark 1

Introduction to This Chapter

The beginning of the Gospel of Mark is not a birth story, as in Matthew and Luke. There is little of a purely biographical interest. Yet certainly Mark means to tell his Gospel by rehearsing the ministry of Jesus. The story of Jesus is enfolded within the Easter faith of the church. And while a concern for Jesus' past should not be excluded, Mark did not intend to produce a "life" of Jesus.

Here is an outline of this section.
   I. Introduction (1:1)
   II. John the Baptist (1:2-8)
   III. The Baptism of Jesus (1:9-11)
   IV. The Testing of the Messiah (1:12-13)
   V. The Theme of Jesus' Preaching (1:14-15)
   VI. The Calling of Disciples (1:16-20)
   VII. The Authority of Jesus Over Demons (1:21-28)
   VIII. The Healing of Peter's Mother-in-Law (1:29-31)
   IX. Summary (1:32-39)
   X. The Leper and the Messianic Secret (1:40-45)

Introduction (1:1)

The Gospel has to do with the Son of God (though some old manuscripts omit the title). This title originated in Judaism as an exalted way of describing the king's special relationship to God. It did not connote divinity

12

originally, though doubtless on Hellenistic or Greek soil it acquired that implication, which it clearly possessed for Mark.

John the Baptist (1:2-8)

The Gospel story begins with John the Baptist, who is here identified by Scripture with the messenger of Malachi 3:1. The quote is actually an amalgam of Malachi and Isaiah 40:3. Mark later suggests the identification of the messenger (John) with the prophet Elijah. In this way John is also taken up into the *good news* (NRSV) (*gospel*) (NIV). He comes as the way-preparer, whose eschatological activity of preaching and baptism opens the way for the ministry of Jesus. John's baptismal work carried the promise of the forgiveness of sins in preparation for the at-hand Kingdom. God's forgiveness of the people as the basis of a new relationship was an expectation in some prophetic circles (see Jeremiah's new covenant prophecy in 31:31-34).

John seemingly has no origin; like Elijah of old he mysteriously *appeared in the desert region* (NIV) or wilderness (NRSV). He demands repentance in preparation for the coming messiah. *The whole Judean countryside* and *all the people of Jerusalem* should not be taken literally; the expressions point to the importance of John's activity as Jesus' forerunner.

The description of John also recalls Elijah and strengthens the picture of him as a wilderness, ascetic figure. His clothing is sparse and his diet is meager, suggestive of preparation for the eschatological age. Among some prophets the wilderness was the place of hope, where God would renew the covenant relationship with the chosen people (see Hosea 2:14-15). John's location there connects him with the expectation of a new era; otherwise, he has no importance apart from his witness to the messiah, whose *sandals* he is not worthy to untie. The expression is proverbial and indicates subordination of one person to another.

The radical difference between Jesus and John is characterized by Mark in verse 8, where John's baptizing activity is limited to *water*. The appearance of Jesus brings a new order signified by baptism with *the Holy Spirit*.

Water was an historic mode of admission to community (as in the Dead Sea Scrolls), or a symbol of purification. It functions as such here in reference to John's activity. The Holy Spirit was the eschatological gift, the sign of the new age at work in Jesus, and could only be imparted with his ministry.

The Baptism of Jesus (1:9-11)

Mark's narrative of Jesus' baptism by John is matter-of-fact. It shows little concern for the question that exercised Matthew: Why was Jesus, the sinless one, baptized with a baptism for sinners? (see Matthew 3:13-17). Mark has a different focus, as he shows in his compact story with its scriptural allusion (verse 9).

Jesus appears just as mysteriously as did John, coming from *Nazareth* of *Galilee* to be baptized by John in the Jordan. Mark's story is not merely a story of human doings; it is that, of course, but intertwined with the human is the divine. Jesus comes for baptism because it is the divine imperative; no explanation is needed for Mark.

Yet it is fair to ask how Mark wishes us to understand this event. What does the baptism of Jesus mean to Mark (and his community)? The *Spirit descending on him like a dove* carries out the announcement of John in verse 8. The origin of the dove as a symbol for the Spirit is unknown; perhaps it comes from the Flood story or—more likely—from the sayings of the rabbis who compared the Spirit of God to a dove. (It is an incidental comment that Jesus came up out of the water; baptism by pouring or immersion is implied, but of no evident consequence one way or another to Mark.)

The theological significance of the baptismal event becomes apparent only in the words of the heavenly voice (verse 11), which acclaims Jesus as the beloved Son. The voice echoes Scripture, partly utilizing the words of the royal Psalm 2, which was composed to honor the enthronement of the king in ancient Israel. In this way Mark proclaims Jesus as the messianic king, with his baptism serving to signify his inauguration as Messiah.

At the same time we notice that the proclamation of Jesus as Messiah is a private affair; the voice speaks only to Jesus. This hidden messiahship is consistent with the picture Mark develops throughout his Gospel, of Jesus as the messianic king whose rule is paradoxically hidden under his role as the suffering one.

The Testing of the Messiah (1:12-13)

Unlike Matthew and Luke, Mark lacks a temptation story, but he refers to the tradition: the Spirit immediately drove him out into *the wilderness* (NRSV) or *desert* (NIV). The harshness of the expression shows its origin in the popular character of Mark's storytelling, and hints at the divinely determined nature of Jesus' mission. It is also conventional in such literature to find a story of testing just after the call-story. So it is here: Having been chosen as the messianic king, Jesus is now put to the test, *tempted* (tested) *by Satan*, though he is assisted in his struggle by the angels who ministered to him. Just how the angels ministered to Jesus seems of no real concern to Mark. Presumably, they provided him with sustenance.

The presence of the *wild animals* (NIV) or *beasts* (NRSV) recalls the theme in prophecy, later developed in apocalypticism, that in the new age the "lamb will lie down with the lion" without harm (for example, Isaiah 11:6-9). Jesus safely dwelling with the beasts implies the coming of the new era.

The Theme of Jesus' Preaching (1:14-15)

Nothing is said yet of the arrest of John, so Mark is anticipating his later story (6:14-29). The *good news of God* which Jesus preaches is not only the gospel about God, but that of which God is the owner—that is, the proclamation of the crucified one. So Jesus, in Mark's view, is a preacher of the Christian message. That is further indicated in the summary of the message: *The time is fulfilled* or *has come* (NIV), *and the kingdom of* God *is near; repent, and believe in the good news.* It is, of course, true that Jesus' own message revolved around the kingdom of God. But Mark has brought Jesus' proclamation into the post-Easter preaching of his church.

The *kingdom* refers to the eschatological rule of God as king over the earth (see the Glossary). No doubt for Mark its ultimate manifestation involves the lordship of Jesus as eschatological Son of man. *Near* describes the Kingdom's presence, without loss of its futurity. That is, the Kingdom is both a present reality and a future expectation.

Repent means to do an about-face, to cease abruptly one's way of life and go in the other direction. To *believe in the good news* is, in Mark's thought, to abandon oneself utterly to trust in the message of Jesus (the "story" that Mark tells).

The Calling of Disciples (1:16-20)

The call of the disciples is meant to be a model of how things are with disciples: when Jesus calls, there is no choice but to leave all and follow him. That is the main import of the story.

Many Markan scenes occur *by the Sea of Galilee. Simon* is Peter who, along with his brother Andrew, is a fisherman (verse 16). The story supports the saying of verse 18, in which *fishers of men* (NIV) or fishers *of people* (NRSV) had probably become an expression in the Markan community for missionaries. It may also go back to Jesus himself.

The call of James and John provides reinforcement of

the point: They even abandon their father Zebedee and leave him to manage the family business along with the *hired men* (hired hands or slaves). Such is the imperative of Jesus' call that all other things are insignificant.

Little is known historically about these disciples. Peter remains the most visible figure, while nothing is known about Andrew. James was martyred in the time of Herod Agrippa (see Acts 12:2), while many traditions about John have been collected, including his authorship of the Fourth Gospel at Ephesus. None of the traditions can be sustained as reliable.

The Authority of Jesus over Demons (1:21-28)

Jesus' first activity is located in Capernaum (verse 21), a city on the shore of the Sea of Galilee, which Mark seems to think of as Jesus' home (see 2:1). Excavations in Capernaum have produced a third-century synagogue, and beneath it the apparent floor of one dating back to the first century, where perhaps Jesus taught *on the Sabbath.*

Mark records that Jesus taught as one having authority, *and not as the teachers of the law* (NIV) or *scribes* (NRSV). Jesus spoke with a directness which did not quote other scribes. Mark illustrates the special position of Jesus with a story of exorcism. The man with the *unclean spirit* is possessed by an *evil spirit* (NIV). The demon recognizes Jesus, for he knows—or they know—that his time is about up (verse 24).

The *Holy One of God* is an unusual title. It probably belonged to the story in its pre-Markan form, and asserted Jesus' special consecration to God. The silencing of the demon(s) is also pre-Markan; it did not originally belong to the secrecy theory, but was a part of the control of the exorcist over the demons. The word *rebuke* (NRSV—translated as *sternly* by NIV) comes from the same old tradition and indicates the subjugation of the evil powers as the Kingdom comes near.

It is typical that the demon causes convulsions and

crying, since it does not depart willingly. The amazement of the bystanders is also a feature of stories of healing (verse 27). What Mark wishes to emphasize is Jesus' *new teaching* and his *authority*, such that his fame spreads throughout the land of Galilee (verse 28). It is strange to refer to the exorcism as a *teaching*, but thereby Mark shows that he thinks of Jesus' work as a unity. The word and deed go together. Both point to Jesus' unique authority as the messianic king whose kingdom is manifesting itself in the conquest of the powers of evil.

The Healing of Peter's Mother-in-Law (1:29-31)

Typical of the Galilean time are the healings and exorcisms. They illustrate the powers of the Kingdom at work in Jesus. So *as soon as they left the synagogue* Jesus enters the house of Peter with the disciples just called, and heals Peter's mother-in-law who was *in bed with a fever* (verses 29-31). Jesus does the messianic deed for one of the disciples. It is of some historical interest that Peter was married (see 1 Corinthians 9:5). There still remains a site in Capernaum which is identified as Peter's house.

Summary (1:32-39)

A summary section follows in which Mark builds up the picture of the successful activity of Jesus in attracting crowds (verse 33) by healing all who were sick or demon possessed (verse 32). At the same time Mark seems to play down the notoriety by having Jesus frequently command silence (verse 34) to those who have received healing. Mark thus picks up from the exorcism tradition a theme which he uses to set out his view of the work of Jesus as paradoxically hidden and revealed (see the Introduction on Mark's themes).

Mark shows us a Jesus who prays often. He usually does so in a *solitary* (NIV) or *deserted* (NRSV) *place* (verse 35), that is, prayer is not to be done for public display. Mark also wishes to emphasize how Jesus needs to escape the pursuing crowds. The disciples follow and find him (verse 37) and report the eagerness of the crowds to see him.

Verses 38-39 indicate Jesus' willingness to be disturbed, and then summarize the Markan conception of Jesus' purpose in coming: *preaching* (NIV) or *proclaiming the message* (NRSV) or *driving* (NIV) and *casting* (NRSV) *out demons.*

The Leper and the Messianic Secret (1:40-45)

Another healing story—disconnected from any of the preceding material—follows in verses 40-45. It, too, continues the buildup of Galilean activity, characterized by the mixture of success and opposition.

A leper (verse 40) would have been an outcast and under the law would not have been permitted ordinary social activity (see Leviticus 13:45-46). It is extraordinary that he even approaches Jesus to ask to be *clean.* The emotion ascribed to Jesus (verse 41) points to the early, pre-Markan character of the tradition. (A more likely textual variant reads "anger" instead of "pity," suggesting Jesus' disturbance at the usual human hopelessness over leprosy.)

The act of healing is briefly described in verse 41*b*. The focus of the story is to be seen in the two following verses (44-45), where Mark again introduces the paradoxical silence theme. The leper is to have his healing certified according to the law (Leviticus 14), though he is not to tell anyone. He ignores that command, with the result that the crowds continue to grow and swarm around Jesus, not even allowing him to enter a town.

By inserting the silence theme here Mark makes a point: The meaning of Jesus' work is not to be found simply in his miracle-working ability, but rather in his role as the suffering one. The "secret" of this king is that he can only realize his rule by dying. Already in the Galilean period Mark begins to set out some qualifications to the picture of the wonder-working Christ.

§ § § § § § §

The Message of Mark 1

Mark's story is not simply a human biography. Certainly Jesus had a human "life," but Mark's message is a form of proclamation, a "gospel" (good news). Even the introduction of John the Baptist serves this proclamation, for John functions to announce in advance the gospel, that is, the coming of good news in Jesus.

There is something surprising in that role. John is hardly the first choice of the respectable. He is a scruffy figure, preaching repentance and demanding baptism. That people go out in response to him is no measure of his personal popularity, but of God's purpose in history.

Also surprising is the presentation of Jesus. The first thing the messianic king does is to submit himself to the humbling experience of a baptism for sinners. And though he is acclaimed as the messianic king, no one else sees it. He then proceeds to call unlikely disciples, and to astonish with his messianic deeds of healing and exorcism. In such ways is the kingdom of God "at hand."

We can sum up these insights in the following way:

§ What constitutes the gospel is not, for Mark, the life of Jesus, but the proclamation-with-passion of Jesus. Yet also for Mark the gospel is a story.

§ God's saving activity on our behalf is never predictable, but always surprises us.

§ What we often consider good news is not necessarily the "gospel of God."

§ The Kingdom is present wherever messianic deeds of healing occur.

§ There are powers of evil in the world to be combatted in the name of the Kingdom.

§ § § § § § §

Mark 2

Introduction to This Chapter

A new section clearly begins at 2:1, though the theme of controversy continues. This new section extends to 3:6, and constitutes something of a unity in itself. It is likely a pre-Markan collection of stories, with some Markan modifications. Chapter 2 embraces the controversy over the healing of the paralytic and Jesus' forgiveness of sins, the calling of Levi and the attached controversy scene over fellowship with sinners and tax collectors, the issue of fasting, and the sabbath debate. In these scenes Mark is continuing to build up his picture of Jesus' ministry as a time of division and debate. The Kingdom does not come without strife and contention.

Here is an outline of this chapter.
  I. Debate over Jesus' Sabbath Authority (2:1-12)
 II. Jesus and the Outcasts (2:13-17)
III. Controversy over Jesus (2:18-28)

Debate over Jesus' Sabbath Authority (2:1-12)

Mark has Jesus return to Capernaum for the controversy scenes that follow. Whether at *home* (verse 1) refers to Jesus' home (as seems likely) or someone else's home, such as Peter's (as seems unlikely), is uncertain. Typically, Mark reports that a large crowd, having heard that Jesus is in town, comes together at his home, so that an enormous press of people is gathered together. The house is so crowded that there is no room for everyone, even *outside* (NIV) or *in front of* (NRSV) *the door* (verse 2). The *word* which Jesus is preaching should be thought of as his message of the Kingdom.

Four men come carrying a paralyzed man or *paralytic* (NIV) or *paralyzed man* (NRSV). The paralytic must have been heavy, if four men were required to carry him. This detail only emphasizes the dreadful condition of the man who is unable to do anything for himself. The compactness of the crowd does not permit the men to enter the house, so they go up to the roof to make an opening to let down the man on his pallet. The scene is clearly Palestinian, where houses had mud-and-branches roofs, accessed by outside stairs, in which a hole could be made. The pallet was the mat-bed of the poor, which could be carried about and therefore *let down* (NRSV) or *lowered* (NIV) (by ropes?) into the main room of the house. (In the typical peasant's house there would have been only a single room.)

The trouble the men go to in order to reach Jesus evokes his evaluation of their faith. Mark seems to mean the faith, in the sense of confidence or trust in Jesus' miracle-working power, of both the paralytic and the men who were carrying him.

Jesus then addresses the paralytic with what seems a strange word: *Your sins are forgiven* (verse 5). It is strange because here Jesus seems to accept the ancient notion that sin and illness were connected, that is, if someone were suffering it was because he or she had committed some great sin. In any case it is apparent that Mark wishes to emphasize Jesus' authority to forgive.

The *scribes* (NRSV) or *teachers of the law* (NIV) (verse 6) were the descendants of Ezra, experts in the interpretation of the law. It is correct that they would question whether anyone had the right to forgive sins save God only. The charge of blasphemy (verse 7) raises the accusation that Jesus here arrogates to himself what can only belong to God. In this way also Mark anticipates the charge against Jesus at his trial before the Sanhedrin (see 14:64).

As Jesus seems to be able to read the faith of the men and the paralytic, so also he perceives *in his spirit* (in himself, verse 8) that the scribes are unfaithful and only have questions. None of their questioning is apparently expressed aloud. We could see this inner perception by Jesus as simply his possession of profound psychological insight, but Mark undoubtedly intends for us to see it as a sign of Jesus' divine status.

Jesus' questions (verses 8*b*-9) are intended to rebuke the faithlessness of the scribes. His question, *Which is easier?* is rhetorical and does not expect any answer. Actually, neither the word of forgiveness nor the announcement of healing is easier, since both are equally part of the authority of Jesus. To proclaim the one is at the same time to proclaim the other.

Verse 10 is grammatically awkward, beginning a sentence but not finishing it. This awkwardness indicates the secondary insertion of the forgiveness-of-sins controversy into an original healing story, probably out of continuing debate with Judaism over the significance of Jesus. Whether Jesus himself claimed the right to forgive sins is yet another issue. Certainly to do so would have arraigned him against the scribes, for whom indeed to raise such a claim would have been blasphemous.

The *Son of Man* is a title derived from the apocalyptic tradition, where it referred to that figure who would be sent by God in the last days to preside over the last judgment, the resurrection of the dead, and the apportionment to human beings of their final destiny. He was, therefore, a figure of great power and authority as God's agent in the end time. The Son of man title underwent further development at the hands of Christian interpreters, where sayings of suffering and activity in the present (as here) were added.

Mark reflects this process and contains all three types of sayings. Whether and in what way Jesus himself spoke about the Son of man, and if he applied the title to himself, is a matter which has occupied scholarship for a very long time, and on which no consensus exists. In this context, Mark clearly wishes to depict the authority of Jesus to act as God's representative in his earthly ministry (*that you may know*, verse 10). Consequently, the healing-word is spoken over the paralytic in verse 11: *get up, take your mat and go home!* (NIV) or similarly in the NRSV: *stand up, take your mat and go to your home!*

That the paralytic goes out *before them all* is a small detail that validates the healing. Typical in such healing stories also is the reaction of the bystanders: they were all amazed and glorified God, *saying, "We have never seen anything like this!"* Mark has secured his point that the Kingdom is making its way into being through such things as the exorcisms, healings, and now also even the experience of forgiveness.

Jesus and the Outcasts (2:13-17)

Jesus once again appears *beside the lake* (NIV) or *sea* (NRSV). Jesus teaches the crowd (verse 13), but it is apparent that Mark's concern lies elsewhere, for he hurries on past this teaching to have Jesus meet *Levi the son of Alphaeus*, who is a despised tax collector. Few people in that society were less popular than the tax collectors, who were usually Jewish citizens hired by Rome—or perhaps, in this case, by Herod Antipas—to tend to the business of tax collection. They got their compensation by fleecing the populace (overcharging) and lining their own pockets. It is understandable that they were despised for their lack of ethics and loyalty, as well as considered unclean because of association with heathen Gentiles.

Jesus does not attempt to justify his call of Levi. The summons to *Follow me* is a life-giving command. The Kingdom is grace, especially to the undeserving.

No attempt is made by Mark to provide psychological

motivations. It is sufficient to say that, when Jesus calls, one must simply answer. Hence Levi *got up and followed him*. Whether this Levi is identical with Matthew the tax collector (see Matthew 10:3) is speculative.

The call of Levi introduces the next scene of Jesus' fellowship with tax collectors and sinners. Mark seems to say that Jesus invited them to his home in Capernaum, since they are in *Levi's house* and apparently are all eating together (*sat at table*, NRSV, only implied in NIV, is literally "reclined," which denotes the posture of dinner guests leaning on their elbows as they eat). Having table fellowship with such persons would render Jesus instantly unclean according to the law. The offense is compounded by the enjoyment evident in the celebration.

The Pharisaic scribes, who were legal experts supportive of the Pharisaic party, direct a question to the disciples (verse 16), though it is Jesus who answers (verse 17). (What the scribes are doing in the house of Jesus is not clear. Are we to assume they were invited also?) Their question is based on the assumption that Jesus' action violates the laws of ritual purity, according to which no scrupulous Jew would eat with someone unclean. Jesus' response is given in the form of a proverb: *Those who are well have no need of a physician, but those who are sick* (NRSV) or translated in the NIV *it is not the healthy who need a doctor, but the sick*. The point is self-evident, and was perhaps a popular way of defending oneself, by saying, in effect, "I'm not the one who has a problem."

Mark—probably even the tradition before him—adds a further saying which makes the central point that Jesus came not *to call the righteous, but sinners*. The emphasis lies not in an assertion that there are some who are already righteous and need no forgiveness, but rather in the call being extended to sinners. Jesus' presence embodies the call of the Kingdom as good news above all to the undeserving, to just those who might not ever expect to belong to the Kingdom.

Controversy over Jesus (2:18-28)

Three more controversy scenes complete this section. (The third is dealt with in the next chapter.) One has to do with fasting, while the remaining two revolve around the issue of sabbath keeping. In every case Mark continues to present the controversial Jesus who embodies the Kingdom, which arouses opposition.

Fasting as practiced by John's disciples and the Pharisees provides the occasion for further dispute. Pharisees regularly fasted as a sign of devotion and purity, and the disciples of John the Baptist also evidently fasted, presumably for eschatological reasons, that is, as preparation for the end time. The accusation is directed to Jesus that his disciples do not fast. The justification is given in the answer of Jesus that the *wedding guests* (NRSV) or *guests of the bridegroom* (NIV) cannot fast while the bridegroom *is with them.*

The emphasis is on the joy of the time of Jesus' presence, which is the presence of the Kingdom, a joy which has no place for the practice of fasting. Obliquely, the sayings go on to provide some justification for fasting in the post-Easter period of the church. That is, fasting is permitted by the loss of the bridegroom. Only *on that day* is it permissible to practice fasting.

Two further metaphors contrast the old ways with the new situation brought about by the Kingdom (verses 21-22). In the first, the image speaks of the impossibility of sewing a piece of unshrunk cloth on an old garment. To do so produces a tear when the garment is washed. The second metaphor describes what happens when new wine is put into old skins: The new wine, giving off gas, causes the skins to swell beyond their limit and burst.

In both cases the point is that the old ways, such as fasting, cannot contain the new experience of the Kingdom. Nothing was more distinctive of Judaism than sabbath observance.

The scene in verses 23-28 renews Jesus' display of freedom toward that institution, showing how the Markan church also regarded the practice of sabbath observance. It is apparent that the post-Easter Christian community felt itself free from observing the sabbath. The community appeals to the authority of Jesus himself to vindicate its position.

The scene is not realistic, in that Jesus and the disciples are wandering through a grain field with the Pharisees trailing along. The artificiality of the scene indicates that its importance lies on another level than the purely historical one. The whole scene is what form critics would call a paradigm, or pronouncement story, whose main purpose is to lead up to the saying(s) at the end.

Verses 23-24 set up the controversy. We presume that the hungry disciples are picking wheat grain (though why they would find raw wheat palatable is a mystery). The criticism of the Pharisees is that the disciples are performing labor (reaping) on the sabbath (see Exodus 34:21). Jesus' defense in verses 25-26 refers the Pharisees to the earlier example of David and his men, who ate the offering of the bread of the Presence in the sanctuary (bread that was usually eaten later by the priests).

The sayings of Jesus regarding who has authority over the sabbath then terminate the scene.

There are problems in the narrative, which conforms only loosely to the original story in 1 Samuel 21:1-6. The erroneous reference to Abiathar as priest (verse 26) instead of Ahimelech (see 1 Samuel 21:1) is perhaps the result of some poor scribal memory. Also, the situation of Jesus and the disciples hardly parallels David and his band of outlaws. And David's eating of the sacred bread seems to have little to do with reaping on the sabbath. The analogy is only broadly made that in both instances the law was set aside in favor of a higher need.

That principle is indeed enunciated in verse 27, where it is set forth that the sabbath must serve human need, not vice-versa. The intent of the sabbath regulation was originally benevolent: No one may be worked more than six days a week. This free attitude toward the sabbath is further authorized by reference to the authority of the risen One (*lord even of the sabbath*, see verse 28).

§ § § § § § §

The Message of Mark 2

In this chapter Mark details how the coming of the Kingdom is a joyous experience bringing freedom and a wholly new situation. At the same time the Kingdom stirs opposition. For there are those who prefer the comfort of the old ways, and who are not prepared to submit to the risk of something new. So the Kingdom brings both joy and hostility.

This opposition and hostility occupy Mark in this chapter, as he sets out just how the Christian experience of the Kingdom induces enmity. Behind this picture lies Mark's concept of discipleship, which necessarily embraces the possibility of pain and suffering in the service of the crucified one.

We can summarize these insights in the following way.

§ Jesus' presence, as the presence of the power of the Kingdom, brings with it the healing grace of the Kingdom. This grace is available to all and especially is grasped by the undeserving and those who have little in the world.

§ To submit to the authority of the Son of man is at the same time to run the risk of rejection in the world.

§ The experience of the Kingdom is not unambiguously joyful, but also brings with it the challenge of living in the face of hostility and opposition.

§ The old ways in the world, such as sabbath observance and fasting, are being set aside in the name of the new freedom of the Kingdom.

§ § § § § § §

Mark 3

Introduction to This Chapter

The controversy scenes which began at 2:1 conclude at 3:6, and a new section is introduced at 3:7. This new section opens with notice again of Jesus' reputation as a healer and its effects, followed by the appointment of the twelve to their mission, the Beelzebul controversy, and the sayings on the unforgivable sin. The section concludes with Jesus acknowledging that a true relationship to him is not familial, but one of following. Mark continues to develop the themes of christology and discipleship.

Here is an outline of this chapter.
I. Controversy over Jesus (3:1-6)
II. Opposition and Success in Galilee (3:7-35)
   A. Jesus' growing reputation (3:7-12)
   B. The choosing of the twelve (3:13-19*a*)
   C. Accusations of demonic possession (3:19*b*-27)
   D. The unforgivable sin (3:28-30)
   E. Jesus' true family (3:31-35)

Controversy over Jesus (3:1-6)

The scene is set in the synagogue again (verse 1; see 1:21), and once more the issue is sabbath observance (see 2:23). Only negative responses to Jesus seem to come in the synagogue. A desperate man is there with a *shriveled* (NIV) or *withered hand* (NRSV), the result of some kind of lengthy paralysis. In a society where manual labor was the rule, such a person would have been in a precarious position, without hope.

The anonymous *they*—presumably the Pharisees (verse 6)—wait for yet another instance of violation of the law. To heal on the sabbath was unlawful for any except a physician in the case of life or death. Thus they sought to accuse him of a punishable offense.

The man with the withered hand is ordered to *Come forward* (NRSV) (verse 3), literally, to *stand up in front of everyone* (NIV)—that is, to be put before the whole congregation. The man is to be the occasion for the presentation of an important principle. Jesus raises the question whether it is lawful on the sabbath to do good or to do harm, to save life or to kill. The question does not really expect a debate to follow, but simply covers all the possibilities of how one might act on the sabbath. Hence the opponents are silent, not simply because they do not wish to argue, but because their theology has no room for an answer. An answer can be given only on the ground of the new situation brought about by the appearance of the Kingdom in Jesus.

This new situation radically qualifies the old ways and, indeed, nullifies them, even including such sacred things as sabbath observance. The silence of the opponents shows that they are utterly unable to think in any terms except the old ones.

Jesus' *anger* and his being *grieved* (NRSV) or *deeply distress*ed (NIV) are signs of an early stage of tradition, where it was still possible to ascribe such human emotions to Jesus. Mark is saying that Jesus found intolerable his opponents' unwillingness to see anything new at work, a sign of their *hardness of heart* (*stubborn heart* in NIV), or willful blindness. The heart is the seat of emotion, the disposition or attitude of the self, and to speak of its hardness is to assert a profound spiritual stubbornness which refuses all evidence of the truth.

Stretch out your hand is Jesus' command which asks the man to demonstrate his faith. He is to reach out to Jesus. When he stretches it out, his hand is *restored*. The use of *restored* suggests that the man's hand was once normal. Mark does not dwell on the act of healing, since he has well established that Jesus can and does heal, and the main focus of the story lies in the controversy over the sabbath law.

The story concludes with the note that the Pharisees and the Herodians consult with one another as to how they might rid themselves of this one who flouts his attitude of freedom towards the law and thus threatens the very structure of society itself.

The Herodians were presumably a party loyal to the Herod family, of which Herod Antipas of Galilee was ruling in Jesus' day, though the greatest of the Herods had been dead for some time (4 B.C.). Just why they would be introduced by Mark here as threatening to Jesus is not so clear; probably this note points to the early, pre-Markan character of the story. In any case, Mark doubtless wants us to see again how many powers came together in negative response to the Kingdom and set out to defeat it.

Jesus' Growing Reputation (3:7-12)

Once more we are brought in verse 7 to the sea. It is a favorable place, where disciples are made and the message of the Kingdom proclaimed. The whole of this next section, through verse 12, appears to be of Mark's editorial construction. It is a summary of Jesus' growing popularity, as he heals and teaches and gathers huge crowds about him. The area from which people come encompasses a large territory, much of which is non-Jewish: not only Galilee, but Judea, Jerusalem, Idumea (which is Edom in the Old Testament), the vague *beyond* (NRSV) or *across* (NIV) *the Jordan*, and Tyre and Sidon (ancient Phoenician cities). In this fashion Mark briefly sketches the attraction of both Jew and non-Jew to Jesus, as the word of his messianic activity goes abroad.

Jesus is forced into a boat (verse 9) because of the crowds pressing in on him, so many has he healed (verse 10). The desperate and the needy cluster about in hope, if only to touch him. Exorcisms are implied, in that Mark now repeats his secrecy theme, telling us how the demons recognize who Jesus is and cry out (through the demoniac) in confession of Jesus' sonship (verse 11). Mark adds the now-familiar editorial comment that Jesus commands the demons to be silent (verse 12).

Here is a clear instance of an identity-silence theme which is of Markan origin. It is Mark's thesis that Jesus appears in possession of all the messianic powers, but that these powers are subordinated to Jesus' mission as the suffering one. Hence what Mark gives us is a paradoxical picture of one whose glory lies hidden under his suffering. Indeed, the glory is only visible to those who have grasped his suffering. The demons see his power, but his true glory becomes visible only in his cross.

The Choosing of the Twelve (3:13-19a)

Jesus then goes up into the mountain, where an important decision must occur: the choosing of an inner group of disciples. The appointment of such a group is by Jesus' choosing (verse 13). No one can volunteer for the position. But one can answer, and the disciples do: *they came to him.* Out of this larger body Jesus chooses twelve to be with him, and to be sent out to preach and have authority to drive out demons. They are to continue the work of Jesus himself.

The symbolism of the Twelve seems clear enough: They represent the twelve tribes of Israel and so are themselves a sign of the new Israel brought about by the presence of the Kingdom. That is no doubt how Mark intends to portray their selection.

The names of the Twelve are taken from tradition, and the various versions in the Gospels do not quite agree with each other (see Matthew 10:1-4; Luke 6:12-16). In addition, textual problems abound in this section, which indicates that later scribes were attempting to harmonize and add in their own versions.

Simon (verse 16) was renamed by Jesus as *Peter*, which comes from the Greek *petros*, meaning *rock*, and goes back to the Aramaic word *kephas*. His primacy in the list probably comes from his having been the first to experience an appearance of the risen Christ (see 1 Corinthians 15:5).

James and John were brothers, the sons of Zebedee, who were called by Jesus early on in Galilee. The significance of the title *Boanerges* (verse 17) is uncertain; even the Aramaic derivation of *sons of thunder* cannot exactly be verified. If allowed, it would suggest some comment on the brothers' fiery temperament.

Andrew and Philip (verse 18) are distinctively Greek names, not altogether surprising in view of the increasingly hellenized culture of first-century Galilee. Of the remaining names, Thaddaeus is missing in Luke, who has instead another Judas (see Luke 6:16). In a number of other manuscripts the name alternates with an otherwise unknown *Lebbaeus*.

Bartholomew, Thomas, and Matthew (verse 18) are also Greek forms of originally Hebrew names, while James the son of Alphaeus is so called to distinguish him from the other James, the son of Zebedee.

Simon the Cananaean (NRSV) seems to be a name derived from the Hebrew *kana*, meaning *zealous* or simply *zealot* (NIV). The word is translated that way in Luke 6:15. Whether this Simon was in fact associated with that revolutionary movement which opposed the rule of Rome and led the struggle which began in A.D. 66 is not known for certain, though that would be the logic of his name. The Zealots as an organized party appear not to have surfaced until after the time of Jesus, when the war against Rome was imminent.

The derivation of the name of Judas (verse 19) is also uncertain, with *Iscariot* possibly meaning *man of Kerioth*, or *assassin*, from the Latin *sicarius* (one who uses a *sica* or dagger).

Little is known of these disciples, and the fact that the tradition is not unanimous even with respect to their names raises the question of how important they were in the life of the early church. Only a few of them, mainly Peter, James, and John, have any particular place in the record, and even that is modest enough. Of course, Judas Iscariot was remembered for his treacherous deed.

Accusations of Demonic Possession (3:19*b*-27)

After the naming of the Twelve, Mark begins to set out just what is involved in responding to the call of this Jesus to be his chosen disciple. It is not a pleasant picture that Mark constructs, for he will show us not only how dark and sinister forces conspired against Jesus, but how even his own family disowned him.

Again Mark has Jesus go *home* (NRSV: The NIV does not specify location of the house). Presumably that means that once more we are taken into Capernaum, though already we have noticed just how lightly the geographical elements are dealt with. And again a large crowd gathers, making impossible any sort of normal activity, such as eating (verse 20). *His family* (verse 21) translates a phrase which might simply mean neighbors or friends as well as family (*those around him*), but likely does have in view Jesus' own relatives.

It is striking that the family members attempt to take Jesus away because they think he is *out of his mind* (verse 21). The family wishes to put Jesus quietly away where he will not be an embarrassment. The story also implies that, since insanity was frequently attributed to demonic possession, the family assumes Jesus to be possessed. In any case it is an unflattering portrayal of Jesus' family, and no amount of re-interpretation can alter the image. It is precisely Mark's point that a disciple must expect what Jesus got, including rejection and ridicule even from those nearest him.

The thought of demon possession leads directly into the Beelzebul controversy, where scribes coming from Jerusalem accuse Jesus of being *possessed by Beelzebul* (NIV: or *has Beelzebul*, NRSV) and of practicing exorcism *by the prince* (NIV) or *ruler* (NRSV) of demons (verse 22). *Beelzebul* means *lord of the flies.* It is likely a term of contempt, representing a deliberate corruption of an original title of a pagan (Philistine) god with the meaning *lord of the house.* The accusation is extremely serious: Jesus is in league with Satan and works his healings by means of satanic power. Thus Mark depicts clearly how far the opposition to Jesus goes.

Jesus answers the critics *in parables* (verse 23). For Mark a parable is any puzzling saying or sayings with hidden meaning, or more broadly, any saying with a comparison. Here the comparison is given in the form of a rhetorical question: *How can Satan cast* (NRSV) or *drive* (NIV) *out Satan?* Obviously he cannot; thus any association of Jesus' work with the activity of Satan is denied. The power of Satan can hardly be invoked to defeat Satan.

The next several metaphors reinforce the argument. Neither a *kingdom* nor a *house divided against itself* will be able to stand (verse 26), since its power is weakened. Likewise, if Satan contends against himself, that must mean that his rule is nearing its end.

Jesus' word contains an irony. He says to the scribes: If what you scribes say is true, then at least we agree that thereby Satan's rule is about over, because the demons are being put to flight. And according to verse 27 the defeat of the demons is the necessary prerequisite to the conquest of Satan's kingdom by the kingdom of God.

Only by first binding the *strong man* can anyone proceed to *plunder* (NRSV) or *rob* (NIV) *his house* (verse 27). The kingdom of God manifests itself as the overcoming of the powers of evil.

The Unforgivable Sin (3:28-30)

There follows one of the most difficult passages in all the Gospels, in brief words which have nevertheless caused a great deal of debate. A similar saying appears in the "Q" source (see Matthew 12:31-32 and Luke 12:10), where blaspheming the Son of man was forgivable, but not blaspheming the Spirit. That saying probably had in mind some distinction between Jesus in his earthly manifestation and in his risen state, when it is clear what is at stake. Mark does not seem to know that form of the saying, but reproduces a version circulating in his community and adds to it his own interpretation.

What this saying originally meant is difficult to determine. The abundance of God's grace is envisioned in verse 28, in that everything is subject to that forgiving goodness: All sins and blasphemies will be forgiven the people. In contrast to that the blasphemy against the Spirit is unforgivable and eternal. *Sins* include all specific acts of disobedience. *Blasphemies* are human acts of arrogance in defiance of God. *Eternal* means not just a long time, but refers to a qualitative separation from God.

The saying seems harsh. Such statements accord poorly with our modern sense of what is tolerable or fair. It seems clear, on the level of the Gospel, that Mark sees the accusation of demonic possession against Jesus as symptomatic of a hardness of heart which is irredeemable. Such an attitude not only fails to discern the importance of the times, but confuses the divine with the demonic and so is hopelessly lost. The saying asserts that there are matters that carry awful consequences, and those who arrogantly set themselves against God had best be prepared to pay up.

Jesus' True Family (3:31-35)

The section that began at 3:7 now concludes with a lesson on the true relationship to Jesus. Mark reports that his mother and his brothers came and called him (verse 31). The picture is again that of Jesus in a house, with a crowd about him, so that these relatives must send a message to him in order to try to draw him away.

But Jesus does not go to them as a dutiful son might be expected to do. Instead he raises a question about who his true relatives are (verse 32). The scene concludes with the lesson Mark is driving home: that the true family of Jesus is *whoever does the will of God* (NRSV) or *God's will* (NIV).

Mark's point is that it may be necessary to abandon even natural family in the service of God, as Jesus himself did. Mark is here staking out some more parameters in discipleship. It is as though he were saying: Do not make any mistake; the cost of following this Jesus may be high, perhaps higher than some are willing to pay, for it may include loss of family relationships.

Mark seems not to know anything of the doctrine of the virgin birth recorded explicitly in Matthew and less noticeably in Luke. Otherwise, it would be difficult to explain his rather rough treatment of Jesus' family as a whole and of Jesus' mother especially. (On Jesus' family generally, see the commentary on Mark 6:1-6.)

The Message of Mark 3

In this chapter Mark continues to set out his picture of the controversial Christ, whose Kingdom comes near wherever acts of grace and healing come near. At the same time this Kingdom implies a new circumstance which overturns many of the old ways and causes an eruption of hostility toward the messenger. The scenes of sabbath observance, family rejection, and accusations of demonic possession all make this point with a powerful impression upon the reader.

We may gather together these lessons in the following way.

§ Acts of kindness and charity may not produce gratitude when at the same time something cherished must be given up. There were some who valued the observance of the law above the restoration of wholeness to the crippled and the maimed.

§ Those who feel themselves called to be disciples must always be prepared to reckon with the possibility that such a life may not be an experience of glory. Even rejection from family members is a possibility.

§ To do the will of God is to be Jesus' true family member.

§ To be insensitive to the presence of the Kingdom is to suffer such a spiritual blindness that the possibility of restoration is foreclosed.

§ § § § § § §

Mark 4

Introduction to This Chapter

In this chapter Mark develops his picture of Jesus as a teacher. There is not much emphasis in Mark on this teaching role of Jesus; rather, Jesus is for Mark primarily the active healer and miracle worker, and supremely the suffering one. But Jesus does teach in Mark, and although there is nothing like the Sermon on the Mount in Mark, there are parables and various sayings about the Kingdom and about discipleship. That process begins significantly in this chapter, though Mark returns to the dynamic, miraculous Christ at the conclusion (4:35-41).

Here is an outline of chapter 4.
I. Jesus the Teacher of the Kingdom (4:1-34)
   A. The parable of the sower (4:1-20)
   B. Warning words (4:21-25)
   C. The seed growing mysteriously (4:26-29)
   D. The simile of the mustard seed (4:30-32)
   E. The importance of parables (4:33-34)
II. Jesus' Command over the Storm (4:35-41)

The Parable of the Sower (4:1-20)

Typically Mark locates Jesus' teaching beside *the sea* (NRSV) or *lake* (NIV). It is also characteristic that a large crowd gathered about him (verse 1), forcing him to move into a boat offshore. It is a vivid scene, with Jesus out on the Sea of Galilee, and a huge crowd attending to his words while seated on the shore.

Jesus teaches them *in parables* (verse 2), which for Mark are puzzles, or stories or sayings with a hidden meaning. The parable that follows is exemplary of Jesus' *teaching*.

The story is about a *farmer* (NIV) or *sower* (NRSV) who *went out to sow* (verse 3). The situation is that of a farmer engaged in the ordinary business of planting his crops. It seems to us that his procedure is curious, throwing seed about so that all manner of bad things happens to it. But that was quite a normal way of sowing: scattering the seed and then plowing it under, rather than first plowing the ground and then planting.

So it is natural that some seed falls along the path, and that the birds come and eat it (verse 4). Such would be the expected fate of some seed that had been thrown out. Other seed falls into *rocky* ground. Because of its shallow root system it cannot withstand the harsh sun, which causes it to wither away (verses 5-6). Still other of the seed suffers a different fate, falling *among thorns* which choke it so that it *did not bear grain* (NIV) or *yielded no grain* (NRSV) (verse 7). Finally, some seed does come upon good soil, and the result is surprising: It grows up and yields a fantastic crop, thirty, sixty, or even a hundred times (verse 8) what was planted.

The final exhortation (verse 9) is a traditional word used in various places throughout the Gospels. It means: Something really significant is being said, so pay careful attention.

On first reading the parable seems not to be terribly striking. What happens to the seed is apparently just predictable. So what is the message here?

We must first make a distinction between what a parable was originally, in the teaching of Jesus, and how parables came to be seen in the life of the post-Easter church. As Jesus used it, the parable was an extended metaphor, a comparison-story that used something out of the ordinary world to say something about the extraordinary, usually in the service of Jesus' message of the Kingdom. What happened to these parables of Jesus in the early life of the church was that they became allegories in which the church saw itself and its own concerns. A parable is not an allegory, even if it has an allegorical feature or two. Rather, a parable is a metaphor and must be looked at as a whole in order to discern its meaning. In an allegory, on the other hand, the message is to be sought in the details of the story which symbolize some spiritual or moral lesson.

This allegorical process goes on already in the Gospels. It can be seen in the very next section of Mark, 4:10-20. Here Mark sets out his theory about parables, and shows that he understands a parable to be an allegory. The allegory reflects the situation of the later church more than it does the situation of Jesus.

A typical literary device of Mark's is to have Jesus explain something to his disciples away from the crowd. So the Twelve and others approach Jesus for an explanation of the parable (verse 10), and receive the remarkable promise that to you has been given the secret of the kingdom of God, but for those outside everything is in parables (verse 11). Still more astonishing is the assertion that the reason for speaking in parables is so that those outside may *indeed look, but not perceive, and may indeed listen, but not understand* (NRSV), or as found in the NIV: *be ever seeing but never perceiving, and ever hearing but never understanding* (verse 12).

The latter statement is taken from Isaiah 6:9-10. It is used here to suggest that Jesus actually meant to hide his meaning from the "outsiders," while communicating it secretly to the "insiders." But that would be an astonishing use of parables, whose purpose is to make something clear, not mask it.

In any case the disciples in Mark do not seem to understand matters any better for having been given an explanation. They continue throughout the Gospel to misunderstand Jesus, and in the end even abandon him. So what can Mark possibly mean?

The mystery (*secret*) of the Kingdom doubtless has to do with its paradoxical hiddenness under Jesus' word and deed, just as the seed in the parable is hidden in the ground, yet mysteriously contains the harvest. The true significance of Jesus and his work is given to the disciples, even though they do not fully grasp it, and cannot until after the Resurrection.

The rather harsh saying of verse 12, asserting the withholding of the revelation from those outside, needs to be seen in light of the passage from Isaiah on which it is based. There Isaiah was reflecting on the futility of his message—ministry to a faithless people. So here, too, the saying reflects the stubbornness and spiritual blindness of the faithless who are confronted with the Kingdom in Jesus' word and deed, yet somehow do not grasp it. It seems as though they were predetermined not to grasp the message, though we surely must allow for some use of hyperbole here.

The allegorical interpretation of the parable follows, after Jesus' rebuke of the disciples for their lack of comprehension (verse 13). The allegorical features are abundant: The seed represents the *word* (verse 14), while the various things which happen to the seed stand for the fate of the word as it is proclaimed in the world. Some persons do not hear the word because Satan *comes and takes away the word* that was *sown in them* (verse 15). Others cannot endure in hard times (verses 16-17), while still others fade away under the influence of worldly desires and pleasures (verse 19). The only seed which multiplies is that which has been sown in good soil.

Originally, the parable probably spoke about the surprising abundance of the Kingdom, which comes in spite of apparent failures and poor beginnings. The future belongs to God, and the parable gives assurance of that future, however unpromising the times look.

At the hands of Mark, or perhaps even of the tradition before him, the parable has been turned into an allegory depicting the fate of the word (the gospel, or the post-Easter preaching of the church). Now it says: Be good soil for the word. What was originally a proclamation directed to those who were skeptical of Jesus' message has now become an exhortation to the church to be receptive to the message.

Warning Words (4:21-25)

The miscellaneous sayings that follow also strengthen this line, though at first verse 21 seems to contradict it. For the point of the rhetorical question about the lamp is that the lamp must be allowed to shed its light. Similarly, for Mark the message of the Kingdom will be known, even though for now only the insiders are admitted to the true understanding.

Verse 22 then sounds like a qualification on verse 11: Though now hidden, all will certainly come to light.

Verse 24a admonishes the hearer to pay close attention to the teaching; it carries lasting weight (verse 24*b*). The promise of still more being given qualifies the language of exact retribution in the first part: Not just what is deserved, but even more is given.

Verse 25 sounds a more threatening note, even with the strange logic (How can you take away from someone who has nothing?). This statement is probably an old proverb expressing irony: The rich get richer, while the poor lose even their prospects. The saying in Mark is meant to be a warning to the community to safeguard what has been given to it.

The Seed Growing Mysteriously (4:26-29)

Again an agricultural image is used to characterize the Kingdom, which is compared to a man scattering seed on the ground (verse 26). The man then goes about his daily routine (sleep and rise *night and day*), noticing the growth of the seed into a plant, though *he does not know* (verse 27). Time obviously passes, and the earth produces of itself, *first the stalk, then the head, then the full grain* (NRSV) or *kernel* (NIV) *in the head* (verse 28). The man has nothing to do with this process, which remains a mystery to him. He recognizes the ripening of the grain, however, and sets to work with his sickle to gather his harvest.

It might seem that a growth process is being emphasized, with the central point revolving around the growth of the Kingdom in the world. But neither Jesus nor Mark had any conception of a Kingdom growing, which is more a modern notion. In any event the simile speaks of the farmer's ignorance of the whole process: He knows not how it all takes place; the earth produces grain. The farmer only knows he must reap the harvest at the right moment, a time he does not determine.

So it would seem that the simile has in mind the mystery of the Kingdom again, which in barely noticeable ways is at work in the world, then suddenly makes its appearance. The *harvest* is a widely known way of speaking about the eschatological age, and is probably so here.

The Simile of the Mustard Seed (4:30-32)

Verse 30 is probably another Markan editorial introduction, having Jesus initiate the teaching with his question about an appropriate metaphor for the Kingdom. The question opens the way for the simile of verse 31, which compares the Kingdom to a grain of *mustard seed* which was known as the smallest seed on earth (verse 31). From this tiny little seed there nevertheless comes something astonishingly large: a great shrub that even can allow the birds to *perch* (NIV) or *make nests* (NRSV) *in its shade* (verse 32).

The point hinges on the contrast being set up between the little seed and the large outcome. The point is not so much that great things come from little beginnings, but rather the emphasis is upon the mystery of how such an enormous conclusion can come from such a small beginning. Applied to the Kingdom, that means: Out of insignificance God will yet bring forth the Kingdom with grand abundance.

The last verse echoes the Old Testament (see Ezekiel 31:6; Daniel 4:12), where similar metaphors are used to characterize the gathering of all nations under the covenant of Israel with God. So it is likely that for Mark there is also in this image an allusion to the coming of the Gentiles into the Kingdom.

The Importance of Parables (4:33-34)

Verses 33-34 then summarize this section on parables and repeat Mark's thesis that Jesus' parable-speaking was itself mysterious and required a private explanation to the disciples. Verse 33 seems to soften the earlier statement in verse 11, since here the word is spoken in parables as people are *able to hear it*, (NRSV) that is, according to their ability to *understand* (NIV). Even so the crowds are not allowed to grasp much, and the deeper comprehension is reserved for the disciples *privately*. Ironically, the disciples do not understand very much even with the help of the private instruction.

Jesus' Command over the Storm (4:35-41)

The focus shifts now from teaching back to action. Before this, Mark has presented Jesus as doer of mighty deeds manifesting the presence and power of the Kingdom, but always in terms of healings and exorcisms. Now for the first time Mark narrates a nature miracle, though he would hardly have recognized our differentiation between the two. Both point to the powers of the Kingdom at work supremely in the activity of Jesus.

The notice of time in the story probably belongs to the story before it came to Mark. The setting presumably is on the same day as the previous teaching in parables, at evening, when darkness would have been coming. The note that Jesus initiated the crossing (verse 35) to the other side indicates that he is fully in command; he gives the order to change the situation.

Some minor problems show in the next verse (36), in that Jesus and the disciples leave the crowds, but it is also said that *other boats were with him* (verse 36). Since these boats have no role to play, their presence in the story is something of a mystery. Perhaps Mark meant to suggest that Jesus never was entirely successful in escaping the crowds.

There is also the curious phrase, *as he was*, which the NIV or NRSV have not known what to do with and simply tagged on, *just as he was*. It might be better to say, "As he was in the boat (already), they took him with them."

The disciples fear for their lives when a storm arises (verse 37). Such storms are not unknown on the Sea of Galilee, coming up with sudden ferocity so that the *waves beat into the boat*, (NRSV) or *broke over the boat* (NIV) threatening to capsize it. The vivid detail emphasizes the absolutely desperate straits of the disciples.

In contrast to the fear and helplessness of the disciples, Jesus is *in the stern*, asleep on a cushion (verse 38). The reference is to the elevated after deck, where normally the helmsman would sit to guide the boat. Jesus' sleeping is indicative of quiet trust even in the midst of terrifying circumstances. The disciples, however, interpret his sleeping as indifference and, rousing him up, reproach him with the question, *Do you not care* if we perish or drown? (verse 38). The question also indicates their own lack of trust and confidence.

Jesus acts before he answers the disciples; their lesson can await their rescue. He *rebuked the wind* (verse 39). The language is similar to that of exorcism; the word used is the commanding word employed by a exorcist to bind evil spirits. The words translated *Quiet* (NIV) *Peace!* (NRSV) *Be still!* also appear to come out of a similar tradition. They may also have their origin in ancient Creation myths, where the creation of the material world comes into being through the conquest of chaos or the watery deep. Certainly Mark's account is reminiscent of such traditions and they have probably contributed something to the shape of this story in Mark.

Jesus' word brings a great *calm*, and the disciples are, like the storm, rebuked by the questions, Why are you afraid? Have you no faith? Even though the disciples are constantly with Jesus, witness his healings and exorcisms, and hear his teaching, they still lack faith, or trust, in Jesus' saving powers. It is only in the face of the Easter experience that the light begins to dawn on them.

The disciples' question, which intends no answer, allows Mark to draw the christological lesson from the story that is implicit in it. *Who* then *is this?* is, in a sense, the question posed by the Gospel as a whole. The disciples are thus properly *filled with great awe*; or *they were terrified* (NIV); intimations at least of Jesus' divine status begin to grow in their consciousness.

§ § § § § § §

The Message of Mark 4

In this chapter Mark has brought before us the Jesus who teaches the Kingdom. The word, the message of the Kingdom, lies hidden in Jesus' activity, just as the seed is buried in the ground. And also like the seed, the word will bring forth eschatological abundance, even if it does not appear to be the case in the present time. From a larger perspective we can summarize these insights in the following way.

§ The activity of God's kingdom is often hidden in the world and available only to those who look with the special seeing of faith.

§ What often seems to us to be a failure of the Kingdom to manifest itself in the world may turn out to be a surprising, enormous victory.

§ None of us should assume that the presence of the Kingdom at work in the world is self-evident; rather, it lies within the ordinary and mundane things of the world. The Kingdom does not show itself apart from the world, but within it.

§ The Kingdom is not at humankind's disposal, but rather is God's Kingdom to make manifest where and when God will.

§ Jesus' saving power, which is the power of the Kingdom, is available not only in the calms of life, but even and especially when the storms seem to prevail.

§ While salvation is not dependent upon human action, faith is the appropriate human response to the saving action of God.

§ § § § § § §

Mark 5

Introduction to This Chapter

This chapter is taken up with three rather long stories: the exorcism of the Gerasene demoniac, the raising of Jairus's daughter, and the healing of a woman with a hemorrhage. Evidently these stories were of more than ordinary significance to Mark, since he uses considerable space relating them.

Here is an outline of this chapter.
   I. Victory over the Gerasene Demoniac (5:1-20)
  II. Raising of Jairus's Daughter (5:21-24a)
 III. Woman With a Hemorrhage (5:24b-34)
  IV. Jairus's Daughter Healed (5:35-43)

Victory over the Gerasene Demoniac (5:1-20)

This vivid story raises some questions concerning details. For example, in verse 2 we read that the demoniac met Jesus when Jesus got out of his boat; yet in verse 6 it is said that the demoniac saw Jesus *from a distance* and ran to worship him. It also appears that verses 14 and 16 could hardly go together, since 16 seems merely to repeat the information given in 14.

These "seams" in the narrative indicate that the story has undergone an extensive history of telling and retelling. The version available to Mark retained many features accumulated over its history, while also allowing Mark to insert his own comment.

The first two verses appear to be a Markan editorial introduction. A textual problem exists in verse 1, where many manuscripts read something different for the location, such as Gedara or Gergesa. The differences are efforts on the part of later scribes/authors to clarify confusion brought about by the (likely original) reference to the *Gerasenes* (verse 1), since Gerasa is some thirty miles away from the Sea of Galilee. The alternative reading of Gedara is not, however, much better, since Gedara is about six miles away, and in either case it is hard to imagine the swine plummeting to their death in the sea. The reference to Gergesa was an effort by Origen of Alexandria (third century) to make a better substitution.

After crossing the sea (verse 1), Jesus disembarks and is met by the man with *an unclean* (NRSV) or *evil* (NIV) *spirit* (verse 2), that is, a demoniac. Demons were often thought to live among the tombs (verse 3), which would also indicate the man's unclean condition according to the law. Naturally also Jesus risks his own purity and that of his disciples by appearing in such a place.

The man's pitiful condition is sharply characterized. Condemned to live among the tombs, his possession is so fierce that *no one could bind* (NIV) or *restrain* (NRSV) *him any more, even with a chain* (verse 3). So many and strong are the demons that the man simply breaks all fetters and chains, and no one is strong enough to subdue him (verse 4). Cast about by the force of his possession, he bangs against the stones (verse 5), bruising himself as he cries out in his desperation.

Just how the demoniac knows who Jesus is, so as to run and worship him (verse 6), is not explained. Certainly it is consistent with Mark's portrayal that the demons recognize Jesus whenever they encounter him, but at the same time they would not have worshiped him. This inconsistency appears in the following verse (7), where indeed the demons inhabiting the man now take the lead and acknowledge Jesus as *Son of the Most High God*, while also imploring him, *Do not torment me* (NRSV: translated in NIV *you won't torture me*. The word translated *swear* (NIV) or *adjure* (NRSV) (verse 7) is the customary word used by the exorcist to address the demon, so here the demons reverse the language and attempt to gain control over Jesus.

Verse 8 seems to interrupt the flow of the story, and was probably inserted (by Mark?) as a correction to verse 7, showing that Jesus already has himself gained power over the demons.

The *name* (verse 9) in antiquity represented the essence of the person, and to know the name was to acquire a certain power over that person. So the point of Jesus' question is to gain power over the demons. The demons' answer, *My name is legion* (verse 9), uses an analogy from the Roman military. A legion was about six thousand men; the point is that the demoniac is inhabited by a large number of demons.

Demons naturally do not wish to be dispossessed of their habitation, and it is a common feature of exorcism stories that demons express that desire. So here they ask Jesus not to *send them out of the country* (NRSV) or *area* (NIV) (verse 10). Instead they propose to be allowed to inhabit a herd of swine (verse 11) which happen to be feeding nearby. The thought of demons taking over swine would be amusing to a Jewish audience, for whom the pig was an unclean animal.

The demons have to beg Jesus (verse 12) to go to the pigs, since now they are under his authority. Jesus agrees (verse 13), the demons come out and enter the swine, numbering about two thousand, and all rush into the nearby sea and drown.

Questions may certainly be raised about this conclusion. How is it that the demons are so easily outwitted, by actually asking to enter the pigs who then rush into the sea? And how can we understand Jesus so casually agreeing to the drowning of these animals?

Such questions arise from our modern concerns, but clearly are of no interest to the original narrator of the story, or to Mark the evangelist. We should recognize the folk-character of the story as it has come down to us, and allow it to speak its message without imposing on it our own reservations. At its core the story wishes to speak of the deliverance wrought by the one who came in veiled authority to make manifest the eschatological Kingdom.

The sequel has to do with the reaction brought about by the news of the healing of this infamous demoniac who could not be controlled by anyone. The swineherds (verse 14) tending the swine relate everywhere what happened, bringing crowds of the curious. These crowds find the demoniac beside Jesus clothed *and in his right mind* (verse 15). Their fear is the classic reaction to the presence of the divine, and they hear the tale of what has happened to the demoniac and the swine (verse 16). The fact that they then begin to beg Jesus to depart from their neighborhood (verse 17) may seem strange, but indicates their fear at the power that Jesus displays, which may be used for good or for evil.

Understandably the man who has been cured also wishes to continue to be with Jesus (verse 18), but Jesus will not allow him to do so. Instead, Jesus orders him to *Go home to your family* (NIV) *friends,* (NRSV) *and tell them how much the Lord has done for you,* and how he has had mercy on you (verse 19). The refusal is not meant to be a rejection; the demoniac has other tasks now to perform in the service of the Kingdom.

This verse (19) and the following one (20) are likely Mark's conclusion to the story. The demoniac does as he is told and goes away to proclaim in the Decapolis how much Jesus has done for him (verse 20). The Decapolis was a collection of ten city-states across the Jordan and of Gentile population. It is fitting from Mark's perspective that the good news of this cure is to be proclaimed aloud in Gentile territory. In all other cases Jesus commands secrecy. The marveling of everyone (verse 20) is a typical element in a healing story.

Raising of Jairus's Daughter (5:21-24*a*)

The scene now shifts again as Jesus crosses once more in the boat to the other side (verse 21). A crowd gathers beside the sea. A certain Jairus, one of the rulers of the synagogue (verse 22), then approaches Jesus with a request. Being a synagogue ruler would mean that Jairus was an important figure in the community; normally a synagogue had two major rulers, the president and the attendant. Jairus falling at Jesus' feet is an act of obeisance characteristic of healing stories.

Jairus's daughter is *dying* (NIV) and is *at the point of death* (NRSV), that is, nearly dead and hopeless. Jesus is implored to lay his hands on her, so that she may be healed. The request assumes that Jesus' reputation as a healer, even one who can restore the dead, is widely known. Jesus consents to Jairus's plea without debate (verse 24).

Woman with a Hemorrhage (5:24*b*-34)

Mark now inserts another healing story before finishing the Jairus incident. Meshing together two stories in this way is typical of Mark's literary style (see 3:22-30; 6:14-29; 11:15-19).

Jesus is followed by *a large crowd* as he goes on his way to heal Jairus's daughter. In the crowd is a woman who has had a flow of blood *for twelve years* (verse 25). A hemorrhage of some sort is presupposed, and according to the law the woman would be unclean (see Leviticus 15:25-30). The lengthy period of her trouble is a feature of such stories in the ancient world, emphasizing the desperation of the circumstances. A similar point is made in referring to the number of physicians she has consulted to no avail, even though she has spent all her substance (verse 26). The point is not to denigrate physicians (who nevertheless did not enjoy a very good reputation in that time), but to emphasize how reduced to hopelessness the woman is, beyond human help.

The woman has heard reports about Jesus (verse 27) and thus hopes to be cured. She makes a timid gesture of faith in thinking that by merely touching Jesus' garments she might be healed (verse 28). This "magical" element is intended to portray the authority and power of Jesus. And indeed such power flows from Jesus, as the hemorrhage ceases (verse 29).

Still more magical is the note that Jesus perceives that *power had gone forth from him* (verse 30), as though such power were merely automatically available.

It would seem that one who recognizes what goes on in other persons' minds would not need to ask, *Who touched my clothes?* But the story is unaware of such problems and wishes to make its own point about the healing authority of Jesus.

The disciples also express incredulity (verse 31), but because there are so many people around that no one can say who touched Jesus. Of course, they misunderstand as usual, for the point of Jesus' question is not simply to know who bumped into him, but who has invoked his power.

Jesus interrupts his movement to look around and see who touched him (verse 32), though the woman has to come forward and speak in fear and trembling (verse 33). After she (presumably) tells him of her dilemma, she is commended for her faith and told to *go in peace*. The last word, to *be healed of your disease* (NRSV) or *be freed from your suffering* (NIV), is actually superfluous, as the woman has in fact already been healed. We should see here the hand of Mark, as he brings this old story illustrating Jesus' messianic power in line with his own insistence on faith as an element in healing.

Jairus's Daughter Healed (5:35-43)

The Jairus story now resumes, with Mark's note that messengers from Jairus's household come even while Jesus is still speaking (verse 35). The messengers report that already the daughter has died and therefore there is no need any longer to trouble Jesus. The message seems callous and the messengers cold; even their allusion to Jesus as *Teacher* is hardly sufficient for the occasion. In fact, their attitude is one of "unfaith," though Mark has no particular interest in condemning them. Instead, Jesus is portrayed as *ignoring* (NIV) them—*overhearing* (NRSV) is also a permissible translation—and proceeding to reassure Jairus that he should not fear, but rather believe (verse 36). Hope still abounds as long as Jesus is present.

Only Peter and James and John (verse 37) are allowed to accompany Jesus, as also is the case at the Transfiguration, in Gethsemane, and, along with Andrew, at the Mount of Olives. The secret is given here to the select inner group. It is doubtful that Mark is making the suggestion that there just was not room for any more in the room where the daughter lay.

Already funeral activities are taking place, with people weeping *and wailing loudly* (verse 38). Public mourning was customary in Palestine, even including the hiring of "official" mourners. Here in Mark the mention of mourning indicates again the finality in human minds of death and the absence of any further human possibilities.

Jesus' rebuke to those who mourn, with the comment that the child *is not dead but* sleeping (verse 39), draws from the assembly a skeptical reaction: *They laughed at him* (verse 40). Jesus' statement has in mind the common metaphor in apocalyptic thought that death was but a temporary condition, described as sleep, before the eschatological Kingdom. This death was contrasted with death as the permanent and final enemy to be overcome (see 1 Corinthians 15:51-57). The mourners' response shows that they cannot yet grasp this possibility.

Jesus sends them all outside and takes with him only his inner group along with the father and mother, who are still faithful and hopeful. It is expected in a healing story that the healer would perform some act such as taking the afflicted person by the hand (verse 41). It is also typical that certain unknown words would be uttered: *Talitha koum* (NIV) or *cum* (NRSV), which is Aramaic and does indeed mean *Little girl, arise* (NIV) or *get up* (NRSV). (The words *I say to you* are an addition.)

Then immediately the little girl arises and walks. The additional statement that she is twelve years old is apparently a parenthetical comment to explain how it is that she walks, especially since the word for *little girl* could have a variety of meanings.

The usual conclusion of a healing miracle gives the reaction of the bystanders, in this case that they are *overcome with amazement* (NIV) or *were completely astonished* (NRSV) (verse 42). The ending is a Markan conclusion, with its expected note about the secrecy theme (verse 43), and the further proof that they should *give her something to eat.*

As history the story presents difficulties for us. The difficulties cannot be surmounted by any amount of rationalization, such as the hypothesis, based on the note that the girl was only sleeping, that she was therefore not really dead but in some kind of coma (diabetic shock, for example). All such theories are really beside the point. Mark wishes to relate a miracle story whose main thrust is that Jesus gives life, that the God whose Kingdom is "at hand" is the God who brings forth life out of death. This Kingdom reigns where the forces of death and darkness are being overcome.

§ § § § § § §

The Message of Mark 5

In this chapter Mark has graphically depicted the overcoming of demonic powers, victory over death, and Jesus' powers of healing. All these are manifestations of the Kingdom as it makes its way in the world. Interwoven in the stories are other typical themes in Mark, such as the invocation of secrecy and the insistence on the response of faith.
These themes may be summarized in the following way.

§ The Kingdom cannot be deterred even by the power of death; hope is a possibility even in the face of apparent hopelessness.

§ God's power is made available at the point where human possibilities are exhausted.

§ Miracles are not merely self-evident, objective events in the world, but require the response of faith.

§ God's mercy is shown not simply to the well-to-do and deserving, but especially to those who are down-and-out and without hope in the world.

§ § § § § § §

Mark 6

Introduction to This Chapter

In this chapter the Galilean picture of mixed success and opposition continues, with the rejection theme heightened by the vivid story of John's death. The miracle stories fill out the other side of Mark's paradoxical picture.

Here is an outline of this chapter.
   I. Rejection of Jesus in His Hometown (6:1-6)
  II. The Mission of the Disciples (6:7-13)
 III. The Death of John the Baptist (6:14-29)
  IV. The Feeding of the Five Thousand (6:30-44)
   V. Jesus' Walking on the Sea (6:45-52)
  VI. The Crowds Coming to Jesus (6:53-56)

Rejection of Jesus in His Hometown (6:1-6)

This first part actually concludes the previous section, which began at 5:1, and it resumes a theme Mark had begun to set out in 4:21.

The note that Jesus comes *to his hometown* (verse 1) refers to Nazareth. The disciples go with Jesus, and the setting is the synagogue on the sabbath (verse 2). We have come to expect from such settings in Mark that controversy will follow. However, it is not the sabbath issue as such that here occupies Mark, but the ongoing debate over who Jesus really is.

The hometowners' questions about Jesus' *wisdom* and

miracles (NIV) or *deeds of powers* (NRSV) are not flattering, but express their unbelief. The villagers also take offense because they know, or think they know, who Jesus really is, since they know all about his origins (verse 3). The question in verse 3 is sarcastic; it expresses amazement that one with such lowly beginnings could rise to any position in the world.

The word translated *carpenter* actually means a *skilled craftsman*. It is unusual to refer to Jesus as the son of Mary, since children were recognized by their father's name. Some commentators have taken this reference to mean that Mark really knew the virgin birth story, but it could also mean that Joseph was no longer alive at that point.

The other brothers and sisters mentioned here are mostly shadow figures in the record. Only James stands out because he entered into the Christian movement in the post-Easter period and assumed a position of leadership in the Jerusalem church. He was known for his deep piety, and died in A.D. 62 as a result of persecution.

About the others little can be said. Tradition has attached the name of Jude to a letter in the New Testament. Nothing is known about the sisters. All were apparently born after Jesus. Some church traditions hold that they were children of Joseph by an earlier marriage, but Mark seems to know nothing of that tradition.

The reception in Nazareth leads to the proverbial comment that *prophets are not without honor, except in their hometown* (NRSV) or as translated in the NIV: *only in his hometown among his relatives and in his own house is a prophet without honor* (verse 4). The saying reflects on the lack of respect caused by familiarity; it is an experience all successful persons have known.

Mark also reports that Jesus could do no miracles (NIV) or deeds of power (NRSV) there (verse 5) with the exception of a few acts of healing. It is typical of Mark that healing must be accompanied by faith. It is also characteristic that a miracle (NIV) is labeled a *deed of power* (NRSV). That is, a miracle is not a proof, but a deed of God to be grasped only in the context of faith. This *unbelief* (verse 6) causes Jesus to wonder at the reception given him in his hometown.

With this scene Mark is not only reporting the absence of faith in Jesus; he is also making another point. All who go the way of Jesus can expect refusal and rejection even from those who are nearest.

The section concludes with the summarizing that Jesus went about among the villages teaching (verse 6). A new section begins in verse 7.

The Mission of the Disciples (6:7-13)

This scene concludes what Mark began in 3:13, with the naming of the twelve apostles. There nothing was said about their special activity, except that they were to do the work which Jesus did. Now Mark finishes that picture. It is typical of his literary style to bring narrative elements together in separated places.

Jesus sends out the Twelve *two by two* to preach (verse 12) and to have *authority over the unclean* (NRSV) or *evil* (NIV) *spirits* (verse 7). The habit of traveling in pairs has analogies in the circle of John the Baptist (see Luke 7:19). The disciples' exorcisms have the authority of Jesus himself and give witness to the approach of the Kingdom.

The instructions to the disciples have been influenced by conditions of missionaries in the Easter period. The impression is of a harsh life: nothing except a staff, *no bread, no bag, no money* in their belts (verse 8). They are allowed to wear sandals, but they may not put on two tunics (verse 9). The bag would have been a wallet, or a beggar's bag. Carrying some money in the belt (or girdle around the waist) was customary. The *tunic* was the garment worn next to the skin; two would have been considered a luxury.

The advice in verse 10 to *stay there until you leave that town* (NIV) or *the place* (NRSV) means that the missionary is not to go about town looking for better quarters. Should a place prove hostile to the missionaries, they are to shake off the dust that is on their feet for *a testimony against them* (verse 11). The practice recalls a traveling Jew shaking off the dust of foreign soil from his feet upon returning to the holy land of Israel. Here the command means that the missionaries have done all they could, and the fate of hostile towns lies not in their own hands.

The disciples then go out and preach repentance (verse 12), cast out demons, and anoint the sick with oil (verse 13). The latter practice is paralleled in Luke 10:34 and in James 5:14, and there are analogies in Judaism to the medicinal use of oil. The oil no doubt symbolizes the inner working of the grace of God. There is no question here of a magical use of this substance.

The Death of John the Baptist (6:14-29)

King Herod hears of Jesus' messianic activity and the rumors it inspires. The notion that Jesus is John the Baptizer (verse 14) awakened from the dead implies that John also performed noteworthy deeds (*these powers,* NRSV or *miraculous powers,* NIV, verse 14). Others suggest, however, on the basis of the expectation expressed in Malachi 3:1, that Jesus is Elijah, while still other rumors point to *one of the prophets of old* (verse 15). The expectation of an eschatological prophet is attested among the rabbis and in the Dead Sea scrolls. Herod seems to subscribe to the John theory (see verse 16).

That Herod had seized John because *of Herodias, his brother Philip's wife* (verse 17) appears to have been only partially true. According to the Jewish historian Josephus, Herodias was not actually Philip's wife, but the wife of another half-brother, Herod. Philip was in fact Herodias' son-in-law, having married Salome, whom

Josephus names as the girl in this story. In any case, it would not have been legal for Antipas to have his brother's wife (verse 18; see also Leviticus 18:16; 20:21).

Herodias' *grudge* against John (verse 19) arose from the Baptist's prophetic denunciation of her illegal marital activity. Her desire to kill him was thwarted by Herod at first because he recognized that John was a *righteous and holy man* (verse 20). The further comment that Herod was perplexed and *yet he liked to listen to him* (verse 20) is puzzling. Mark probably meant to suggest a split in Herod's character; he was attracted to John, but at the same time was mystified by him.

According to verse 21, the opportunity came for Herodias to rid herself of the bothersome prophet on the occasion of Herod's birthday. All the high court officials were invited, as well as high-ranking military officers and others of influence. It was a grand setting for the violent scene that followed.

The dancing of Herodias's daughter (verse 22) led Herod into a lust-inspired promise to swap even *half of my kingdom* (verse 23). The daughter's question provided the right moment for Herodias, who wanted the head of John the Baptist *on a platter* (verses 24-25). The added note about the platter only accents the irony; the dinner guests would now be served the head of John the Baptist.

Herod seemed not to have the stomach for the request. But because of his *oaths* and his *guests* (verse 26) he could not refuse without losing credibility as to his word and his rule. The order was given, and *immediately* resulted in the beheading of John. The gory present was given to the girl, who then gave it to her mother (verse 28). And while Mark reports no further on the disposition of John's head, he has finished his story. It remains only to note that John's disciples *came and took his body, and laid it in a tomb* (verse 29). A contrast with Jesus is intended. Both were laid in a tomb, but only Jesus came forth.

Why does Mark devote so much time to this story? For

one thing, the story embodies the sharp malevolence of worldly powers to the messengers of God. And, further, John's destiny foreshadows Jesus' own way of the cross. There is point and counterpoint in the story. Both John and Jesus perish at the hands of evil forces in the world, though only Jesus overcomes these forces.

The Feeding of the Five Thousand (6:30-44)

The apostles return from the mission that began in 6:7, report on their activity (verse 30), and are invited by Jesus to come away and *rest* for a while (verse 31). The scurrying of the crowds about Jesus prevents even normal eating, so Jesus and the disciples go away in the boat (verse 32) to escape. Yet the crowds will not leave Jesus alone, so they run on foot to get ahead of Jesus and the disciples (verse 33). We may wonder how all these people seem to know where Jesus and the disciples are going. Mark has not carefully integrated the story with its context.

The throng awaits Jesus as he lands on the shore (verse 34). After a long day the disciples approach Jesus and suggest that this is a *remote* (NIV) or *deserted* (NRSV) *place* (verse 35), and that the people ought to be sent away to get something to eat. Jesus' answer tests their faith: *You give them something to eat* (verse 37).

The disciples respond with a practical comment about the huge amount that would be required to feed so large a crowd. Two hundred denarii would have been the average daily wages of 200 working men. Jesus ignores their question which, after all, only illustrates their misunderstanding. Nevertheless, the disciples are given something to do: *Go and see* how many loaves there are in the crowd (verse 38). They do this task with some diligence, and report that there are two fish as well.

Jesus orders people seated by *hundreds and by fifties* (verse 40; see also Exodus 18:21). Nothing hidden is intended. The point is that Jesus is in command of every detail, including the seating on *green grass*, or a comfortable place.

The blessing and the breaking of the loaves would have sacramental overtones to Mark's readers, while the participation of the disciples suggests a concept of ministry. The satisfaction of all (verse 42) emphasizes the fullness of the work Jesus does; nothing is lacking. The twelve baskets left over (verse 43) not only indicate the abundance of Jesus' feeding, but also correspond to the twelve tribes of Israel. Together with the other feeding story in Mark 8:1-10, this story makes a point about the inclusiveness of the church. The report about the number who ate is not meant to be taken literally, but rather to indicate that a very large group was fed.

Jesus' Walking on the Sea (6:45-52)

This story was connected with the feeding story in the pre-Markan tradition. Here too is disclosed the exalted Lord in his manifest power and deity. Even the sea is subject to his command, as in the stilling story, since he treads upon it without slipping in.

No reason is given for Jesus' sending the disciples to the other side of the sea; he acts out of his own authority. Bethsaida was located on the north shore of the Sea of Galilee. Jesus dismisses the people, while he himself goes into the mountains to pray (verse 46). For Mark, Jesus prays not only as a model of piety for the church, but also because in prayer lies his renewed strength.

The disciples are on *the lake* (NIV) or *sea* (NRSV), while Jesus remains on the land by himself (verse 47). A wind storm arises and the rowing becomes difficult. Jesus then comes to them *at the fourth watch of the night* (NIV) or *early in the morning* (NRSV) (about 3:00 in the morning). Mark is narrating a rescue story, but a puzzling statement follows: He meant to *pass by them* (verse 48). Jesus' desire to go by the disciples does not mean he wishes to see them drown, but that his action is calculated to provoke their response, hopefully one of faith and trust.

The disciples again do not grasp the significance of the situation, but mistake Jesus for a ghost (verse 49). In their fear they cry out and are answered by Jesus, *Take heart* (NRSV), or *Take courage!* (NIV) *it is I; do not be afraid!* The language is that of divinity; the story is an epiphany and manifests Jesus in his true identity. At the same time the rescue motif is reintroduced in that, when Jesus gets into the boat with the disciples, the wind ceases (verse 51). Jesus' presence brings assurance against the storm.

The disciples are *completely amazed* (NIV) or *astonished* (NRSV) (see verse 51). Mark comments on their lack of understanding by referring to their hardened hearts and their failure to perceive *about the loaves* (verse 52). Again in evidence is the misunderstanding of the disciples. Apparently the miraculous feeding showed them nothing. And now in the walking on the sea they see only a ghost.

The Crowds Coming to Jesus (6:53-56)

A typical summary concludes this section. The boat lands at Gennesaret (verse 53), a plain that actually lies south of Capernaum and quite a distance away from Bethsaida. Again we notice the freedom with which geographical elements are treated.

When Jesus disembarks, immediately the people recognized him (verse 54). They begin to bring him the sick to be healed. The crowds follow Jesus wherever he goes, in whatever village or town, hoping that they might touch *even the edge* (NIV) *fringe* (NRSV) *of his cloak* (verse 56) to be made well. Thus Mark emphasizes how powerfully divine forces flow through Jesus.

§ § § § § § §

The Message of Mark 6

In this chapter Mark carries forth the familiar theme of rejection, this time by Jesus' own hometown people. This theme is developed into the idea of worldly hostility, as seen in the story of the death of John. The mission of the disciples shows how any disciple may also expect to suffer rejection. Even so, the powerful Christ is present and provides for all his disciples' needs and comes to them when the storms are rough.

We can summarize these points in the following way.

§ What is familiar to us is too easily taken for granted, and we cannot see in it the activity of the divine.

§ Only faith can see where the Kingdom is at work in the world.

§ To undertake mission in the name of Jesus is to run the risk of rejection in the world.

§ There are powers of evil in the world which greet the proclamation of God's rule with death and hostility.

§ In the face of adversity Jesus is there to satisfy with his word.

§ § § § § § §

Introduction to This Chapter

Mark now focuses attention on the question of the relationship of the Christian community to Judaism. Here issues as to the binding nature of the oral law arise. In Judaism there existed a long tradition of oral interpretation of the requirements of the law of Moses. This oral law was considered as binding as the written law, at least in certain circles (Pharisaic). The question would have been raised among Jewish Christians as to whether they, too, must also observe this oral law. These scenes in Mark are meant to answer those concerns. Whether the issues go back to the time of Jesus himself is not always as clear.

In addition, the assertion of freedom from the oral law raises the question as to the nature of this new community which Mark represents. The healing stories in this chapter are addressed to such questions.

Here follows an outline of this chapter.
   I. Ritual Defilement; the Corban Issue (7:1-23)
  II. The Status of the Non-Jew (7:24-30)
 III. Healing Outside Galilee (7:31-37)

Ritual Defilement; the Corban Issue (7:1-23)

Appropriately, the Pharisees and some of the scribes (verse 1) should appear to raise the issue of the binding nature of the oral law. Eating with *unwashed* hands was not a health issue, but a religious one. Whether there existed in the time of Jesus an expectation that one should wash hands before eating, in order to be considered ritually pure, is not clear from the available sources. The earliest references are found in the Mishnah (see the Glossary), but cannot be traced back beyond about A.D. 100. Some aspects of this controversy may stem from the post-Easter period.

Mark explains for the benefit of the non-Jews in his community the requirement of the *tradition of the elders* (verse 3), which refers to the oral tradition of legal interpretation by scribes or experts in the law. The phrase *when they come from the marketplace* (NIV: which is implied in the NRSV, verse 4) may also be taken as referring to food purchased there, that is, they do not eat anything from the marketplace without purifying themselves. If we follow the translation in the Revised Standard Version, we would have to assume Mark was saying that merely mingling with a crowd in the marketplace rendered a person unclean.

The washing of various vessels also has reference to ritual purity. We know from the Dead Sea Scrolls that ritual purity was a matter of importance to groups such as the Essenes. It symbolized acceptability before God.

The Pharisees direct their accusation toward the disciples (verse 5), in itself a clue that the controversy had its importance and perhaps even its origin in the early church, rather than in the time of Jesus himself. However, the authority of Jesus is invoked to settle the dispute. Scripture was especially useful in such debates with Judaism, so the text from Isaiah 29:13 is quoted to show that the Pharisees do not adhere to God's commandment, but follow instead the *traditions of men* (NIV) or *human tradition* (NRSV) (verse 8). The Isaiah text spoke of hypocrisy; presumably Mark means that the Pharisaic doctrine of ritual purity is allowed to override the actual words of the commandments, in the name of obedience. It is clear that for Mark and his community there is no longer any sense of being bound by the oral law.

The statement of verse 8 provides a link to the next section. The Corban controversy illustrates how the Pharisees have rejected the commandment of God by reinterpreting its requirement. The commandment to *honor your father and your mother* (verse 10) was taken to mean that children were obligated to provide for the physical necessities of their parents when their parents no longer could do so. However, this commandment might come into conflict with the legal seriousness of keeping an oath (see Deuteronomy 23:21-23).

According to that law, some portion of a child's support was *Corban, given* or devoted to God. In such a case a child might claim relief from the obligation of parent support. Hiding behind such a vow is what is condemned as *making void* (NRSV—or in the NIV nullifying) *the word of God* (verse 13).

The whole scene from verses 1-13 leads up to the striking pronouncements in verses 15-23, addressed to the people in general. The principle that Mark wishes to set out really addresses the issue of ritually pure or impure food, not hands or even what is Corban. The logical connection here is very weak, but clearly Mark is concerned to set out how his Christian community distinguishes itself from Judaism. And the basic principle enunciated here is extremely radical, from the perspective of Judaism, that is, that all foods are permitted. The ground of such a claim is that thoughts and intentions are more important than dietary regulations. Such a statement would be impossible for a person steeped in the law and the scribal tradition, in which many foods were prohibited and considered unclean.

In typical fashion Mark has Jesus leave the crowd (verse 17) and provide a private explanation for the disciples. Of course, they do not understand it anyway (verse 18), since they are still under the power of the old era. Mark interprets the word of Jesus about the non-defiling character of food to mean that thereby all foods are *clean* (verse 19) for the Christian.

The concluding comment (verses 21-22) elaborating what may be considered truly defiling is an interpretation of the basic principle. Such lists of vices—and virtues also—were fairly common in the Hellenistic world, and are especially notable among teachers of Stoic ethics. It seems probable that this list in Mark has some association with that practice.

Evil thoughts (NIV) or *intentions* (NRSV) are condemned because they give rise to evil deeds. The word translated *fornication* (NRSV) is a general term for sexual immorality (NIV) of various sorts, while *theft, murder, adultery, and greed* (NIV) or *avarice* (NRSV) all directly reflect the Ten Commandments.

The other vices in this catalogue are more general human traits that cause social problems. *Wickedness* (NRSV) or *malice* (NIV) is any kind of general evildoing; *deceit* is dealing treacherously with one's neighbor. *Licentiousness* (NRSV) or *lewdness* (NIV) refers to sensual overindulgence, especially of a sexual nature, while *envy, slander,* and *arrogance* (NIV) *pride* (NRSV) are traits which destroy relationships. *Folly* (NIV) *foolishness* (NRSV) is a lack of both moral and intellectual sense, and the emphasis is on the moral side.

Since these things come from within (verse 23), they are what is truly corrupting. Thus Mark sets out the new freedom of the Kingdom which dispenses even with the old law. Here ritual purity has become insignificant; what matters is ethical uprightness.

The Status of the Non-Jew (7:24-30)

The scene now relocates to largely Gentile territory. The area of Tyre and Sidon (verse 24) embraced all of

Phoenicia. That Jesus *entered a house* raises questions with some commentators (Whose house? How did he know anyone was there?). Mark is unconcerned with such problems. His interests are clear in the statement that Jesus did not want anyone to know he was there, *yet he could not be hid* (verse 24). We recognize the paradoxical combination of hiddenness and openness. The stage is set for an encounter with a Gentile, among whom also Jesus' reputation has spread.

There appears an unnamed woman whose daughter is possessed by *an unclean* (NRSV) or *evil* (NIV) *spirit*. The woman seeks an exorcism, having presumably heard of Jesus' reputation. It is significant that she is a *Greek* (NIV) or *Gentile* (NRSV), *a Syrophoenician* by birth (verse 26), and not, therefore, among the chosen people.

Jesus hesitates to comply with her request to cast the demon out of her daughter. His comment to her about taking the children's bread and throwing it to the dogs (verse 27) hardly seems kind. The saying no doubt expresses a certain Jewish narrowness: They are the children; the Gentiles are the dogs. Considering that Jews did not care much for dogs, the saying sounds like a Palestinian proverb denigrating the place of Gentiles.

The woman's clever response (verse 28), however, gains Jesus' admiration. At least the crumbs ought to go to the non-Jew, she suggests. Jesus commends her for what she says (verse 29), with the result that her daughter is healed. The woman then goes home and finds her daughter well and the demon gone (verse 30).

The story is best understood when seen from the perspective of the later church and its issue of Jew and Gentile together. Jesus' seeming reluctance to deal with this pagan woman points to the uncertainty with which the first church moved into the Gentile mission. The modest commendation which Jesus gives the woman—no characteristic mention of her faith—also shows the difficulty the church had in dealing with the non-Jew.

Yet at the same time Mark is clearly telling us that Jesus himself approved the inclusion of even the pagans in the Kingdom.

Healing Outside Galilee (7:31-37)

No motivation is given for Jesus' movements in the Gospel. None need be, since Jesus operates according to his own imperatives. His passage from Tyre and Sidon to the Sea of Galilee into *the region of the Decapolis* is a strange route. No one would go from the west coast of Palestine to the Sea of Galilee by passing through the Decapolis, which was on the eastern side of the Jordan River. Perhaps Mark wishes to have a Gentile setting for the scene that follows.

A man who is deaf and has a speech impediment (verse 32) is brought to Jesus for healing. Small wonder that he cannot speak plainly if he is deaf! Jesus takes the man aside (verse 33), in accord with the Markan theory of secrecy. The rather strange manipulations that follow, with Jesus putting his fingers into the man's ears and touching the man's tongue with spittle, have parallels in the religious practices of the time. Special actions of the healer are sometimes described, and in this case obviously something other than speech is necessary, given the man's deafness.

Jesus' *looking up to heaven* (verse 34) points to the actual source of his healing power, while his sighing denotes his anguish at the man's pathetic condition. It is also not unusual in healing stories to find the use of "magical" words, or formulas known only to the healer. In this case Mark depicts Jesus using a tongue not well known to Mark's community, as the word *ephphatha* is Aramaic and means *be opened*. The cure of the deaf-mute (as he probably originally was) is shown by the mention of his speaking *plainly* (verse 35).

Mark does not, as was his usual custom, mention the faith of the one cured (neither in the case of the deaf-mute nor in the case of the Syrophoenician woman). He does not thereby mean to say that faith is not expected of Gentiles, but rather that his story has its focus elsewhere. That focus lies in the attitude of Jesus himself, and his general inclusion of the non-Jew in the new community. That new community is brought into being by the appearance of the Kingdom in Jesus.

The final section is Mark's editorial conclusion. The secrecy theme reappears, with the note that Jesus commands all to tell no one (verse 36). The acts of miraculous healing are played down by Jesus, lest anyone get the wrong impression about his messiahship. He is not the glorious miracle worker who comes to make life easier, but the one who comes to take up a cross and to summon persons to a life of servanthood.

The paradox in Mark's secrecy theme is seen in the further comment that Jesus' admonitions to silence only produce a zealous telling (verse 36). The astonishment of the crowd (verse 37) is a feature of miracle stories that we have observed before. It remains true for Mark that Jesus *has done everything well*, even though above all his special work is to be seen in his suffering journey to the cross.

§ § § § § § §

The Message of Mark 7

In this chapter Mark sets out the new freedom of the Kingdom. This freedom extends especially to the old law and its oral interpretation. Christians are not bound to the law, and do not observe the ritual regulations regarding proper washing, nor even the dietary regulations. Mark's community has obviously separated from Judaism and finds little value in continuing to observe all the old ways. Indeed, the scenes in this chapter show that Mark's church appealed to the Jesus-tradition to undertake a sharp criticism of such things as the oral law of Judaism.

This debate gives rise to the further question of the makeup of this new community that no longer observes the law. Mark does not speak his last word on this issue in this chapter. However, the scenes that take place outside Judea, in Tyre and Sidon and the Decapolis, are symbolic of the new community that is generated by the Kingdom and that does not exist on the basis of national identity or belonging to a certain people.

These insights may be summarized in the following statements.

§ The Kingdom gives rise to a new freedom that overturns all the old ways and will not submit to the rule of the law.

§ The presence of the Kingdom in Jesus brings into being a new community that is based on the free grace of God, and not on any personal qualities of deserving, family, race, or national pride.

§ What matters in the behavior of the members of the new community is not external adherence to a set of regulations, but internal matters of thought and intention.

§ § § § § § §

Mark 8

Introduction to This Chapter

This chapter begins with what seems to be a repetition of a former incident, the miraculous feeding story. A somewhat mysterious explanation of the two events follows, preceded by the signs controversy and followed by a healing story. Then Mark breaks truly new ground with the significant scene occurring at Caesarea Philippi. For the first time the disciples seem to catch on to who Jesus is, though they still have lessons to learn in the meaning of Jesus' messiahship. Discipleship and its expectations are the dominant themes throughout the chapter.

Here is an outline of this chapter.
I.   Feeding of the Four Thousand (8:1-10)
II. Pharisaic Questioning (8:11-13)
III. The Disciples' Lack of Understanding (8:14-21)
IV. The Man Healed in Stages (8:22-26)
V.   The Way of Jesus and His Followers (8:27–9:1)
     A. Peter's confession at Caesarea Philippi (8:27-30)
     B. First prediction of Jesus' passion (8:31-33)
     C. The meaning of discipleship (8:34–9:1)

Feeding of the Four Thousand (8:1-10)

This story appears to be a duplicate of that in 6:30-44. It is probably an earlier version of the same event, since here the crowd is smaller and is fed on larger amounts.

The tendency of such stories, handed on orally, is to magnify the details. However, in retelling it in yet another version Mark obviously wants the reader to see it as significant.

The setting is vague; *during* (NIV) or *in those days* (NRSV) is a generalizing introduction. A large *crowd* is necessary to the story, as is the desert setting (verse 4). The motivation for Jesus' action is again his compassion (verse 2) for the people who have been attending to his word for three days with nothing to eat. The further comments that they could not get home without fainting, and that some have come a long way, supply vivid details that bring out Jesus' concern.

The disciples' question as to how anyone could possibly feed such a crowd *in the desert* (NRSV) or *remote place* (NIV) (verse 4) again illustrates their failure to understand, in that they certainly have before them the previous feeding. Jesus ignores the disciples' skepticism. His question about the number of loaves they have (verse 5) is meant to involve them in the miracle. Certainly Jesus does not need the disciples to supply information to him.

Details of this version differ from the earlier one. Here there are seven loaves and *a few small fish* (verse 7). There is no command to organize the crowd into companies of certain numbers, no looking up into heaven as the bread is blessed. This is a simpler and less developed version.

The crowd is commanded simply to sit down on the ground as one might at a meal (verse 6). Jesus' action with the seven loaves is normal before eating; he gives thanks and breaks the bread so it can be distributed to the crowd by the disciples. The word for giving thanks is the root of the term by which the sacrament was referred to in the early church (*eucharisteomai, to give thanks*, from which came the word *eucharist*). The other term Mark uses here in connection with the fish (*blessed*, NRSV or *gave thanks* NIV, verse 7) also has sacramental associations (see 1 Corinthians 10:16). However, we ought not to think that the Markan community used fish sacramentally. The parallels are not intended to be exact, but merely suggestive.

The crowd eats and is *satisfied* (NIV) or *filled* (NRSV) (verse 8). The implication is that Jesus feeds abundantly at his table. The leftover baskets emphasize this point; even more could be fed. The number *four thousand* (verse 9) is not in itself significant; Mark says only *about* four thousand. That means a big crowd.

Afterward Jesus sends the crowd away and gets into a boat to go with the disciples into the district of Dalmanutha (verse 10). Mark does not mean that Jesus is wearied with the crowd, but that there are other things to be concentrated on, especially now the understanding of the disciples. Dalmanutha is totally unknown to us, and the manuscript tradition shows efforts by scribes over the years to make corrections.

Pharisaic Questioning (8:11-13)

It is typical of Mark's narrative style, as we have noticed before, to sandwich unrelated material between two parts of the same story. Here he places the motif of conflict with Pharisees before returning to the themes introduced by the feeding story.

The Pharisees come (in Dalmanutha?) and begin to *question Jesus* (NIV) or to *argue with him* (NRSV) (verse 11). They ask for a *sign from heaven*, that is, a miraculous proof of Jesus' message and credentials. Jesus' disdain of such requests shows in that he *sighed deeply*, and refuses to give any such sign (verse 12). Mark knows that miraculous proofs are not available for faith; faith has no props, so to speak, not even in the form of miracles.

That Jesus does miracles is unquestionable, but the miracles do not accredit him. Miraculous events have an ambiguous quality in any case. Even Jesus' disciples do not grasp Jesus' significance because of miracles, while his opponents could credit his works to the activity of Satan.

Some lessons for the disciples follow. In the boat the disciples notice that they have brought no bread (verse 14), prompting Jesus to warn them about the *yeast of the Pharisees and that of Herod* (verse 15). Yeast's working was considered mysterious. Hence it could become a metaphor for something with hidden or even corrupting power. The latter probably accounts for its prohibition in connection with the Passover celebration. Jesus' word is a warning against the corrupting ways of the Pharisees or of Herod.

The disciples cannot get the point even though they discuss it among themselves (verse 16). Their comment means: We don't even have any bread, so why is he talking about leaven? Jesus then interrogates them mercilessly. His questions (verses 17-18) are intended to shame them for their lack of understanding. Put otherwise, Mark does not relent in his forceful portrayal of the incredible thickness of the disciples. And yet many besides the disciples also have had difficulty comprehending just what is going on here.

Jesus asks the disciples about the number of baskets which were left over in the two feedings. But his question to them is left open and unanswered. *Do you not yet understand?* becomes the question addressed also to the reader of the Gospel. Certainly the disciples show by their comments and questions that they have not yet arrived at the faith which truly comprehends. Even in the face of such remarkable experiences as they have had they fail to grasp what Jesus is about.

They do not grasp the significance of the twelve and the seven as experienced in the two feeding stories. The twelve would seem to be a symbol of Israel and its twelve tribes. A clue to the seven may rest in Acts 6:1-6, where seven was the number of the Hellenistic or Greek-speaking element in the early church. Mark would see in it that both Jewish and Hellenistic Christians can come together at the feeding table of the suffering and risen one, who provides for all needs abundantly.

The Man Healed in Stages (8:22-26)

Bethsaida (verse 22) was a fairly large town, and Mark has often given it as a locus of Jesus' activity. Here Jesus encounters a blind man brought to him to be healed. Jesus' actions seem strange, in that he takes the blind man out of the village (verse 23). Mark's intention is to preserve the secrecy motif.

Again customary actions by the healer occur; Jesus spits on the man's eyes and lays his hands upon him (verse 23). At first the blind man seems not to see clearly; men *look like trees, walking* (verse 24). Jesus then lays hands on him a second time, and the man sees everything clearly (verse 25).

Mark is not saying that this was a particularly hard case, so that Jesus had to apply two doses, so to speak. Rather, the healing of the man in stages is symbolic of the spiritual journey which the disciples are making, and about which Mark has just been commenting. Like the blind man, they too come to see, but only in stages. This coming-to-see of the disciples is what will occupy Mark in the next section.

The act of healing ends with the familiar command to secrecy. The man is sent home and ordered not even to enter the village, that is, not to allow any questions to arise about how he was healed, but to keep to himself.

Peter's Confession at Caesarea Philippi (8:27-30)

The scene which now takes place in the vicinity of the villages of Caesarea Philippi (verse 27) is certainly a crucial one in Mark. A past generation of scholars sought to find in this scene a turning point in the life of Jesus himself. The theory was that Jesus here began to introduce his disciples to the novel idea of the messiah who must suffer, and that he went thereafter to Jerusalem to implement his vision.

We are much less certain today that this was the case historically with the ministry of Jesus. What does seem clear is that Mark the theologian-evangelist wishes to convey something important in rehearsing this significant scene. Caesarea Philippi may be a turning point, but only in the theological picture Mark constructs, not necessarily within the life of Jesus.

Caesarea Philippi was a city built by Philip, son of Herod the Great, in honor of himself and Caesar. A pagan city, its non-Jewish origins may still be seen today in the grotto of Pan which lies nearby. It is significant for Mark that this first open acknowledgement of Jesus should occur outside Judea.

Jesus initiates the conversation by asking about the rumors the disciples have heard regarding his identity. The disciples respond in terms of popular beliefs: *John the Baptist, Elijah,* and *one of the prophets* (verse 28). Reference is apparently to a belief that John had been resurrected, as Herod earlier had said (6:14); Elijah's appearance was anticipated before the end of time on the basis of Malachi 3:1, while the expectation of a prophet (like Moses) also formed part of eschatological beliefs in that time.

Jesus acknowledges none of these titles, but presses on to ask the disciples for their evaluation: *But who do you say that I am?* (verse 29). Peter answers on behalf of all the disciples, *You are the Christ* (NIV) (Messiah, NRSV). The Markan secrecy theme follows, in Jesus' charging them to tell no one about him (verse 30).

Here Peter seems to grasp for the first time what is going on; he knows who Jesus is. Yet only part of Mark's picture has been sketched. That is why Jesus makes no immediate response to this confession (quite in contrast to Matthew's version, where Peter is first blessed; see Matthew 16:17-20). The issue now is not whether Jesus is the Messiah, but what kind of messiah he is.

First Prediction of Jesus' Passion (8:31-33)

Jesus then tells them that *the Son of man must suffer many things* (NIV) or *undergo great suffering* (NRSV) (verse 31). These many things include his rejection at the hands of the authorities, his ultimate death, and his resurrection. The first of three predictions of the passion of Jesus is found here, as Jesus now sets out to define just what the concept of messiahship really means.

The traditional title of messiah is not used by Jesus, as Peter had done. Instead, Jesus speaks of the *Son of man*, certainly a more enigmatic title. Originally—though there is still dispute—the Son of man was a figure expected in connection with the last days, a highly authoritative, eschatological figure whose main function was to be God's representative at the final judgment. His role was to apportion the fate of human beings in the end time.

Whether Jesus himself spoke this way is a matter of debate among the scholarly experts. At the Caesarea Philippi scene, Mark uses the title to introduce the new thought of the messiah who comes preeminently to give up his life for others.

Jesus says this *plainly* (NIV) or *openly* (NRSV) (verse 32), so that there will be no mistaking it. The disciples, of whom Peter is the representative, do not misunderstand this time; they get the point, only they cannot bear it. Thus Peter *began to rebuke him* (verse 32). Rebuke is a strong word, normally applied to an exorcist's control over a demon. Peter is treating Jesus as a man possessed. In turn Jesus *rebuked Peter* (verse 33) and, in even stronger terms, called him *Satan*. Jesus then commands that Peter be no longer before Jesus as a temptation to a wrongly directed messiahship.

This exchange between Peter and Jesus is uncommonly powerful. In it Mark is relating to his own community the true nature of Jesus' messiahship: that Jesus is no popular hero, or even merely a glorious miracle worker, but the one whose role is disclosed only in his suffering and death.

At the same time this christology has profound implications for discipleship. To follow such a one implies a willingness to go the way of the cross, to expect suffering, and not glory and power. Here Mark's concept of discipleship emerges profoundly, and serves to refute any view which reckons only on a glorious, miracle-filled life in the Kingdom here and now.

The Meaning of Discipleship (8:34–9:1)

Mark's intention is clearly set out in the section that follows, and in which the demands of discipleship are made clear. Jesus calls together the multitude with his disciples (verse 34) for the instruction that follows. Mark's concern is to indicate that the teaching that follows is intended for an audience larger than merely the inner group of disciples.

Jesus speaks conditionally of discipleship. The condition, grammatically speaking, is assumed to be true. If indeed anyone wishes to be Jesus' disciple—and let us assume he or she does—then it follows that self-denial and cross-bearing are expected (verse 34). To deny the self does not mean to disparage human life and its possibilities; on the contrary, it means that only in the abandonment of all worldly security and prior claims of the self can true life be found. Only in giving is there receiving.

The same point is raised in the question about what profit there is in gaining the whole world while losing life, or about what a man can give in return for his life (verse 37). Life that is devoid of meaning cannot be reclaimed by the possession of all the goods of the world. Nothing can replace a sense of purpose and destiny in life. Discipleship bestows that sense, and only in the renunciation of all other claims can life be filled with meaning.

Two somewhat loosely connected sayings conclude this section. One is the threatening saying in verse 38. The saying has in view the eschatological judgment, and it asserts that the eschatological judge, the Son of man, will disown all those who have disowned him. The saying works on the basis of the old law of retribution, whereby punishment was meted out in exact proportion to the crime. This law hardly seems compatible with the spirit of Jesus' genuine teaching, as, for example, in Matthew 5:38-48.

To be *ashamed* seems to reflect more the situation of the Markan church as it faced the outsiders who mocked its following of the crucified one. The saying warns and—indirectly—promises, with its assertion of the glory of his Father *with the holy angels* (verse 38).

This section actually concludes at 9:1. The versification of the Bible does not always coincide with its logical breaks; versification was added many years after the original texts were prepared.

The striking saying of 9:1 is loosely tied to the preceding, in that both speak of the eschatological Kingdom. Here the bold promise is made that *there are some standing here who will not taste death before they see that the kingdom of God has come with power. With power* refers to the visible action of the Kingdom and contrasts with its hidden presence in the earthly work of the messiah. But the saying stands as hope and promise for the time and the church of Mark, as it may still stand today.

§ § § § § § §

The Message of Mark 8

In this chapter Mark has brought his picture to a preliminary climax. The second feeding story, with its accompanying lessons for the disciples, emphasizes the identity question and points to the continuing failure of the disciples to understand. Both Pharisees, who ask for proofs, and the disciples, who ponder why they have no bread, fail to see what is going on around them. The disciples are like the blind man who only came to see in stages. In this way Mark introduces that process of coming-to-see which is disclosed, at least partly, at Caesarea Philippi.

In summary we can develop these themes as follows.

§ Understanding of who Jesus is cannot be gained from observation of marvelous events; such events have an ambiguous character that opens them to various interpretations.

§ Miracles are called "signs," that is, pointers to something significant, but not proofs. Miracles cannot give a proof for faith, for they require precisely the interpretation *of* faith in order to be meaningful.

§ Jesus is not the messiah by popular acclamation; as the popular messiah he was a failure. He was instead the suffering messiah, the one acknowledged by Peter but still misunderstood.

§ There can be no true quality of life which is not prepared to give itself up. Servanthood is the condition for finding life.

§ § § § § § §

Mark 9

Introduction to This Chapter

Mark's story of the Transfiguration opens this section. Following the prediction of the Passion, a contrast is inserted that has in view the coming glory of Jesus. Yet it is not a different Jesus with which Mark wishes to present the reader, but still the suffering, crucified one. This is seen in the exorcism story that follows, and in the second prediction of the Passion. The continuing failure of the disciples remains in view in this chapter, as they show themselves unable to deal with the concept of servanthood or of an appropriate faith.

Here is an outline of this chapter.
  I. The Transfiguration (9:2-8)
 II. The Elijah Expectation (9:9-13)
III. Jesus' Exorcism (9:14-29)
 IV. Second Prediction of the Passion (9:30-32)
  V. Lessons on Discipleship (9:33-37)
 VI. Friends and Enemies of Jesus (9:38-41)
VII. Admonitions to Disciples (9:42-50)

The Transfiguration (9:2-8)

After *six days* Jesus went with an inner group of three disciples up to a high mountain, where he was *transfigured before them* (verse 2). The six days may suggest a close connection with the preceding scene, or may be drawn from the analogy of the Moses tradition (Exodus 24:16), where the sacred mountain was covered with a cloud (God's presence) for six days before Moses could approach.

Peter, James, and John are the usual three who comprise a select inner group allowed in on special events. This limited participation of disciples serves Mark's secrecy purposes.

Jesus' transfiguration may recall the shining of Moses' countenance (see Exodus 34:29) as he returned from the mountaintop, but also has parallels in the apocalyptic literature as a description of the condition of the saints in the end time.

We are not told about the nature of Jesus' transfigured body. That Jesus' garments became glistening, intensely white (verse 3) is symbolic of his divine status and recalls again the clothing of the righteous at the end time. It is also typical that angels are similarly described.

The appearance of Elijah with Moses may seem a strange element, but these two held a special place in apocalyptic writings. We have already noticed that Elijah became an object of speculation because of his unusual end (see 2 Kings 2:9-12); likewise rabbinic tradition spoke of a translation of Moses directly into heaven. These two characters represent the Law and the Prophets, which are gathered to Jesus and which find their fulfillment in his work. What they are talking to Jesus about is left unsaid; Mark simply wishes to emphasize Jesus' authoritative position.

Peter's brash proposal, *let us make three shelters* (NIV) or *dwellings* (NRSV) (verse 5), again represents a misunderstanding. The reference is to the practice of dwelling in booths, or temporary tent-like structures of brushes, at the pilgrim festival of Booths or Tabernacles. Tabernacles celebrated the wilderness wandering in Israel's history. Peter erroneously wishes to remain in a condition of revealed glory, and to place Jesus in a pantheon of the glorious saints, such as Moses and Elijah. But that cannot be; the mountain must be descended and the way to Jerusalem followed.

Mark comments on Peter's apparently pointless

remark in verse 6, and slightly excuses Peter by apologizing that he *did not know what to say* because he was afraid. Fear is awe in view of the divine presence.

In the Old Testament the *cloud* is a symbol for God's presence. The voice from the cloud, *This is* my beloved *Son; listen to him*, is deliberately reminiscent of the baptismal story. It is a reconfirmation of Jesus' status, spoken now openly in this revelatory situation. Just before going on to Jerusalem Jesus' unique personhood receives divine confirmation. The experience ends suddenly (verse 8), and the vision disappears.

Matthew refers to this event as a *vision* (NRSV; NIV translates it as *seen*) (see Matthew 17:9); many modern commentators have seen here a Resurrection-appearance story projected back into the ministry of Jesus. No one approach seems to do justice to all the elements in the story. Mark seems to present here the glorified Jesus, in a kind of point-counterpoint to the preceding Passion predictions. The Transfiguration anticipates the Parousia and gives hope that, in spite of the Passion which lies ahead and in spite of the unrelenting failure of those who go with Jesus, the purposes of God are working out. This is the other side of Mark's paradoxical picture of the hidden and revealed messiahship of Jesus.

The Elijah Expectation (9:9-13)

Verse 9 is Mark's editorial comment, involving the secrecy theme. The disciples are sworn to silence until the *Son of man had risen from the dead*. Here Mark depicts the actual course of events, in that the glory of Jesus became evident only in light of the Resurrection. The lack of understanding on the part of the disciples is again shown in that they say nothing, but keep asking about the meaning of rising from the dead (verse 10). Still they only want to see the glory of Jesus and cannot assimilate the necessity of the path of pain and death.

The appearance of Elijah on the mountain raises the

question of his significance. The scribes say that *first Elijah must come* (verse 11). The "first" implies that the expected prior coming of Elijah, based on Malachi 4:5, is to prepare for the Day of the Lord (Day of Judgment) and is therefore an act of mercy, meant to warn the people. Jesus replies that Elijah does come first *to restore all things* (verse 12). The restorative role of Elijah is connected with his work of purification in preparation for the Day of Judgment. This work is actually assigned by Mark to John the Baptist, who preaches judgment and practices a baptism of repentance, as preparation for the coming of the messiah. This activity is also closely linked, therefore, with the Son of man who will suffer and be treated with contempt (verse 12).

The conclusion that Elijah has come (verse 13) seems clearly to refer to John the Baptist, who fulfills that role. It is more problematic to locate where it is written about Elijah that he would suffer a fate like John's.

Jesus' Exorcism (9:14-29)

Jesus and the inner three come to the disciples who are engaged in a debate with scribes while a crowd (verse 14) is gathered about. The amazement of the crowd has to do with its recognition of Jesus in his divinely given authority. The people greet him (verse 15); nothing is said of the others who also have come down from the mountain. The focus of the story is on Jesus.

Jesus initiates the conversation by directing toward the disciples a question regarding their debate with the crowd (verse 16). The answer comes by way of a complaint from someone in the crowd who has brought to Jesus his son to be cured (verse 17). The description of the son's illness depicts one who is demonically possessed. The evil spirit seizes him, throws him down, and he foams at the mouth and becomes rigid (verse 18). The symptoms resemble strongly one who is having epileptic seizures, and such illnesses could be ascribed to demonic possession. The vividness of the description intensifies our awareness of the son's condition.

In Jesus' absence the disciples were asked by the man to help his son, but they could not respond (verse 18). The disciples' failure extends to incompetence; they are part of a *faithless* (NRSV) or *unbelieving* (NIV) *generation* (verse 19). Jesus' rhetorical questions then show his disgust at this generation's unwillingness to give itself in the kind of trust which can overcome even the demons. But his compassion for the possessed boy is nevertheless evident in the command, *Bring him* (NRSV) or *the boy* (NIV) *to me.*

The evil spirit recognizes Jesus and causes the boy to convulse and roll about on the ground, foaming at the mouth (verse 20). Strangely, Jesus delays the healing and carries on a conversation with the father. The discussion sounds like a doctor with his patient, with the father recounting pathetically how long the child has been ill, and his recurring symptoms (verses 21-22). The point of these details is not so that Jesus can make a proper diagnosis; rather, these are elements of popular story telling which heighten the dramatic intensity.

The father tentatively implores Jesus, in his desperation seeking any help for himself and his family (verse 22). Jesus seizes upon that conditional plea, and rebukes the father's halfhearted approach. Instead Jesus emphasizes faith's limitless possibilities (verse 23), and evokes from the father the honest cry, I believe; help my unbelief (verse 24). His outcry at least puts him on the road toward faith. Now he knows, as everyone knows, that faith has the character of a gift and cannot simply be conjured up.

Mention of a crowd *running* together (verse 25) at this late point in the story, after we have heard from the beginning about the crowd (verse 14), raises the probability that two stories have here been loosely joined together. One, showing Mark's special handiwork, dealt with the incompetence of the disciples, while the other was originally an exorcism story. It is not clear what connection the exorcism has with the crowd's coming together; perhaps Mark means that Jesus acted before the crowd assembled in order to prevent the demon from attacking still others.

The commanding word is lengthier than usual, and the demon is addressed as *deaf and mute spirit* (NIV). This is translated in the NRSV as *you spirit that keeps this boy from speaking and hearing* (verse 25). We may wonder how a dumb and deaf demon of any sort could be commanded; but the story comes out of popular narrative where such questions are really immaterial. The focus is upon the authority and power of Jesus as healer, such that this most vicious of demons vanishes after causing further convulsions (verse 26), and leaving the boy seemingly dead. Jesus' final act of kindness is to take hold of the boy and lift him up (verse 27). Not death but new life is his state.

Characteristically, the disciples ask Jesus *privately* (verse 28) why they were unable to effect a cure. The answer has historically posed such a difficulty that the manuscripts show various scribal efforts to improve upon it. Not only *prayer* (verse 29) is required, but fasting as well, according to other old, but not likely reliable, textual traditions.

Why then only prayer? Prayer is an act of faithfulness, and precisely that quality is what the disciples lack. Their failure measures their lack of faith, which finds expression in their incompetent praying as well.

Second Prediction of the Passion (9:30-32)

Mark now has Jesus passing through Galilee incognito (verse 30). He wants to avoid arousing a crowd. The stress lies upon instruction of the disciples. He teaches them again about his coming passion, once more with use of the *Son of man* title (verse 31).

The note that after three days he will rise contrasts with a variant tradition that the Resurrection was on the third day (see Matthew 16:21). The tradition of three days belongs to the empty tomb story, which had not attained a fixed form at the time of the writing of the Gospels.

It is not surprising that the disciples do not understand the saying, and that furthermore they are *afraid to ask him* (verse 32). The ignorance of the disciples grows out of their miscalculation about the nature of Jesus' messiahship; their fear grows out of a chilling sense that perhaps they have understood after all.

Lessons on Discipleship (9:33-37)

The setting at *Capernaum* is familiar. The general location *in the house* (verse 33) is characteristic of Mark. The disciples are interrogated with respect to a conversation they were busily engaged in on the way (verse 33). Their silence (verse 34) indicates their guilt, because they were discussing *who was the greatest* (verse 34). The thought of the disciples talking about which of them was the greatest is ironic.

The fact that Jesus sat down *and called the twelve* indicates a certain solemnity; something important now needs to be taught. Teachers normally sat when they taught, but Mark is also emphasizing the significance of the sayings that follow. Indeed, the word about being *last* of all *and servant of all* (verse 35) may be taken as the primary lesson in discipleship to be found in Mark. The saying speaks of that reversal of ordinary values that must characterize the sons of the new Kingdom and those who would go the way of the crucified one. True greatness, as the disciples do not yet know, cannot be found in adding up one's social status or worldly standing. It is only available where the vision of servanthood prevails.

The object lesson is found in the example of the child (verse 36) whom Jesus puts before the disciples and takes *in his arms*. This altogether human act of Jesus supports the saying that reception of such a child in the *name* of Jesus is tantamount to reception of Jesus himself and of the one who stands behind his work (verse 37). The word used for *child* indicates a very young child, even an infant, and therefore speaks of one who is dependent. To attend to the needs of such a one—*to welcome*—is to assume the role of the servant. It is to grasp what is involved in the call of Jesus.

Friends and Enemies of Jesus (9:38-41)

This section consists of miscellaneous sayings, generally about discipleship, with some minimal narrative framework. The saying in verse 40 is the heart of the first section (verses 38-40); the narrative of John reporting about the man casting out demons (verse 4) merely provides a setting. Jesus forbidding the disciples' unwillingness to have anyone invoking Jesus' power is justified by the saying he that *is not against us is for us* (verse 40). Mark's church, faced with a hostile world, would have found comfort in such a word. Friends are where you find them.

The added saying in verse 41 is loosely tied to the scene, in that it promises *reward* (eschatological) to anyone who is kind to those who *bear the name of Christ* (NRSV), that is, Christians or *those who belong to Christ* (NIV).

Admonitions to Disciples (9:42-50)

Miscellaneous sayings follow, held together by no single theme, but by the catchword principle (a word in one saying evokes the same word in a somewhat different saying).

Probably the *little ones* (verse 42) are connected in Mark's thinking with the preceding ones who bear the name of Christ. So the warning is directed against any who attempt to cause the disciples of Jesus to go astray. The thought of causing others to fall leads directly into the warnings concerning other things that might give similar offense.

The command in verse 43 sounds rigid. But it

illustrates the terrible consequences of going astray. For the end is either entering life maimed or going to Hell with two hands. The word translated *hell* is literally *Gehenna*, the town dump outside Jerusalem. The word translated *unquenchable* (NRSV) or *the fire never goes out* (NIV) is the word *asbestos* in Greek. So the *asbestos fire* is the one that simply will not be put out.

Verse 44, which speaks of the undying worm and unending fire (found in the King James Version) is generally omitted in the more modern versions. Similarly, certain phrases comprising verse 46 are usually omitted on the ground of lack of textual support in the most reliable ancient versions.

Originally the passage probably went on to make the same point as in verse 43, using the metaphors of *foot* (verse 45) and *eye* (verse 47). Verse 49, which graphically depicts the conditions of a typical refuse dump, probably gave rise to the inserted verse 44. The connection of verse 49, other than the catchword *fire*, is not at all clear. The manuscripts show many different efforts to interpret it. To be *salted with fire* (verse 49) is to be sprinkled, like salt, with fire—a very vivid mixture of images for characterizing the time of judgment or persecution.

The salting-with-fire saying connects by catchword with more salt sayings, all directed to discipleship. The point of salt that has lost its *saltiness* (verse 50) is that it is no longer useful. Perhaps Mark has in mind salt that has been corrupted with sand and is no longer pure. So it might also be with disciples who are not careful with their discipleship.

The last saying urges the disciples to *have salt in yourselves, and be at peace with* one another. Here is a more positive use of the salt image. It suggests that being "salty" is a good thing, as indeed *salt is good* (verse 50). Salt is not a necessity, like bread; but it lends a certain "spice" to life. It puts some taste into things. So the disciples are to be the livening force, and, as such, they will be *at peace*, or reconciled with each other.

§ § § § § § §

The Message of Mark 9

The dominant theme in this chapter is discipleship. Even the Transfiguration, which opens the chapter, contains lessons for the disciples. They are to see that, though the cross cannot be surmounted, beyond it does lie hope. The Transfiguration gives a glimpse of Jesus in his resplendent glory. If there were no such expectation in Mark, the pervasive emphasis on the cross and the crucified one would cause the story to be depressing.

Again the disciples are taught the importance of servanthood. Yet they continue to misunderstand, even when given special instruction. Their dullness extends to spiritual incompetence. They cannot rouse the demons; they do not even know how to pray. Indeed, their prayerless existence is a sign of their faithlessness.

These insights can be summarized in the following way.

§ There is hope beyond the suffering and pain to be found in this world. The God of the cross does not mute that pain, but takes it up into the hope of glory.

§ To follow Jesus is to learn his way of servanthood.

§ To be kind to one's neighbor, who may be like a needy child, is to be kind to Jesus at the same time.

§ § § § § § §

Mark 10

Introduction to This Chapter

In this chapter Jesus makes the transition from Galilee
to Judea, on his way to Jerusalem. Yet along the way
Jesus does not do anything different. He continues to
teach generally and deliver utterances on the subject of
discipleship. The third prediction of the Passion follows,
as the cross event comes more and more to the
forefront. At the same time the demands of discipleship
grow stronger and more urgent. And, paradoxically, the
disciples themselves grow even denser in their
misunderstanding of that demand.

Here follows an outline of this chapter.

Marriage and Divorce (10:1-12)

Jesus now departs Galilee. He goes to *the region of Judea*
and across the Jordan (verse 1). The itinerary is
peculiar. The reverse makes better sense, and many old
manuscripts correct Mark at this point. Of more
concern to Mark are the crowds that gather to Jesus.

Pharisees appear as if by magic—they always seem to be around when a controversy is brewing—and they interrogate Jesus to test him (verse 2). Their question is about the legality of a man divorcing his wife. The form of the question is hardly Pharisaic, since there was no issue among Pharisees regarding the lawfulness of divorce. The only issue was the proper ground for divorce, and there was debate over that question among the experts. The way in which the question is put, therefore, really reflects the discussion within the Christian community.

Jesus' answer at first directs the questioners to the Mosaic law (verse 3), which did indeed allow a man to *write a certificate of divorce*, (NIV) or *dismissal* (NRSV) and to put his wife away (verse 4; see Deuteronomy 24:1-4). Jesus' interpretation of the reason behind the permission of divorce is that it was given because their *hearts were hard* (NIV) or their *hardness of heart* (NRSV) (verse 5), that is, a concession arising from human stubbornness and unwillingness to submit to the genuine will of God. On the other hand, Jesus locates God's will in marriage in the very act of Creation itself. What God intended from the beginning of Creation (verse 5) was to join male and female together in a oneness. This intention to form a one-to-one relationship is seen in the creation of the male and female genders.

Consequently, *a man shall leave his father and mother and be joined* (NRSV) or *united* (NIV) *to his wife, and the two shall become one* (verse 7). The emphasis is upon the union created by the marriage bond, and it is intended that all other relationships shall be subservient to that bond.

The interpreting comment, *so they are no longer two but one* (verse 8), emphasizes this unity attained in the marital bond. Being one, the two cannot be broken apart (verse 9) or divided again.

This prohibition of divorce seems harsh to a society such as ours, where the dissolution of marriage is often little more than a minor inconvenience. It is no doubt the case that Jesus himself spoke this way, and that also for Mark this regulation expresses the higher standard expected of disciples. But what lies behind this more elevated expectation?

First, it is noteworthy that the prohibition is addressed to men. That is because women did not have the right of divorce in Judaism. Their only recourse in a bad situation was to leave their husbands. So the effect of the command is to limit the action of males with regard to their wives. Women are not to be treated like chattel, or mere property to be dispensed with at the man's whim.

Second, this command of Jesus envisions pure obedience to the will of God, which is to effect a unity in marriage. Whoever enters marriage thinking that divorce always provides a way out already shows that he has not grasped the obedience contemplated by the way of Jesus.

Matters are not made any easier in the next section, where the disciples, as is customary in Mark, ask Jesus for an explanation (verse 10). Jesus' reply not only affirms the sanction against divorce, but gives the divorced parties who remarry the status of adulterers (verse 11). Here Mark already has modified the saying of Jesus to apply to his mixed-Gentile situation, in which women did have the right of divorce. (The most original form of Jesus' saying is likely to be found in Luke 16:18.)

Few churches today observe this word of Jesus literally. Its difficulty does not nullify what Jesus had to say on this subject, but at the same time there is no compulsion to turn his words into a new legalism. That would indeed be a strange practice for a community that claims to preserve the way of one who challenged Pharisees over their unrelenting insistence on the letter of the law.

Receiving the Kingdom (10:13-16)

The disciples again provide a contrast for the sayings of Jesus by *rebuking* (NIV) or speaking *sternly* (NRSV) to those in the crowd who were bringing children to Jesus (verse 13). Jesus repudiates the disciples' actions with the saying about not hindering the children (verse 14). The saying sounds backwards, as though the children should belong to the Kingdom. How can the Kingdom belong to such as these?

While the Kingdom is not a possession, nevertheless there are those who can come to enjoy it with the appropriate attitude. And that attitude is what is recommended here: openness and willingness to receive, which is characteristic of children. That is what is involved in receiving the Kingdom *like a little child* (verse 15), and what earns the blessing of Jesus (verse 16).

The Prior Demand of the Kingdom (10:17-22)

Jesus now is traveling to Jerusalem. An anonymous man runs up to him, and in the posture of a supplicant, addresses Jesus as *Good Teacher*. This address is corrected by Jesus with the counter-question, *Why do you call me good? No one is good but God alone* (verse 18). This tradition goes back to Jesus, and it reflects his insistence that only persons whose intentions are pure can be called good.

Jesus then addresses the question posed by the man as to what he must do to *inherit eternal life* (verse 17). First the man is directed to the commandments. It is as though Jesus says: There is no mystery in finding eternal life; be obedient to what you already know. The man protests that he has observed these commandments since his youth (verse 20), but evidently has not found satisfaction.

Jesus sees more deeply into the man. That Jesus *loved* him does not imply emotional feeling. The word used (*agape*) means a concern for the other without regard to merits or worthiness. Jesus saw the man's possibilities, and knew that the one thing he lacked was freedom from attachment to his possessions.

What the man is told to do (verse 21) cuts across all our natural instincts to get and gain. And yet it is directed at this particular man and not held up as a general rule for everyone. Mark intends this word of Jesus to illustrate the dire cost of discipleship. That is especially evident in that the man could not accept Jesus' word (verse 22). Not all can hear the call and its price exacted on their lives.

The Requirements of Discipleship (10:23-31)

Severe words on the expectation of discipleship now follow. Jesus' looking around (verse 23) emphasizes the solemnity of what is about to be said. The disciples' amazement at his words is not surprising, since popular belief held that material possession was a sign of God's favor. Though Jesus' form of address is caring (*children*), he here reverses that popular thinking. Instead, he emphasizes how hard it is to enter the kingdom of God (verse 24).

The hyperbole speaks of the near impossibility of a wealthy person entering the Kingdom. There is no gate in Jerusalem called the Camel's Gate, in spite of efforts aimed at finding one. The image comes out of Jesus' imagination.

The disciples' astonishment only grows with these words, so they ask with bewilderment, *Who can be saved?* (verse 26). Their entire world is coming down around them. Jesus' answer makes it clear that no amount of human striving can attain the Kingdom (verse 27). But it is possible with God, whose Kingdom it is.

The final verse in this section is a saying that found widespread favor in the early church, and was attached to many different contexts. Mark has placed it here in order to emphasize that no one should be complacent about his or her place in the Kingdom.

The Third Prediction of the Passion (10:32-34)

Mark reminds us that Jesus and the disciples were on the road, *up to Jerusalem* (verse 32). The fact that Jesus was walking ahead of them indicates his purposefulness, as he makes his way to his destiny in Jerusalem. The amazement and fear of those with him show their sense of foreboding at what lies ahead in Jerusalem. It is not a way they would choose for themselves.

When Jesus *took the twelve aside* again (verse 32), it points to the significance once more of what is being said (in verse 33). The delivering of the Son of man is a technical term in the Passion narrative, but never is there any speculation about who does the handing over. Everything happens by divine determination, though at the same time human responsibility is not diminished.

The great detail in this third and last prediction of the Passion emphasizes Jesus' attempt to penetrate the dullness of the disciples. The effort was apparently in vain, as the following scene shows.

The Disciples Argue Over Greatness (10:35-45)

James and John appear with a bold request, prefaced by the even bolder statement asking Jesus to *do for us whatever we ask* (verse 35). The reader of Mark would likely think them out of line, and the other disciples also express the same thought (verse 41). Yet Jesus gives their request a polite hearing (verse 36) in order to teach some important lessons.

With characteristic irony Mark shows the disciples asking about special places of preference in Jesus' kingdom (verse 37). Jesus has just finished speaking about the terrible things that must happen in Jerusalem; the disciples only want to think of glory.

Jesus' answer is at first a rebuke (verse 38). These two do not grasp the implications of their request. There is no glory without first passing through the way of the cross. So Jesus asks them, Are you able *to drink the cup that I drink?* The cup-and-baptism imagery points again to the cross.

The disciples answer Jesus' question rather lightly: *We are able* (NIV) or *we can* (NIV) (verse 39), they say, although it will be apparent later that they have miscalculated. Jesus affirms that they will share his destiny (verse 39), in a saying that likely reflects the experience of the post-Easter community as it confronted a hostile world in its preaching mission.

The specific request of the two disciples is not denied, but Jesus does deny that the conferring of seats in the Kingdom is his prerogative. Rather, it is for those for whom it has been prepared (verse 40). Election to places in the Kingdom is God's gift.

The other ten disciples become indignant (verse 41) when they hear of James's and John's power play. They are angry not because of the nature of the request, but because someone else attempted to get ahead of them.

Jesus' calling the disciples to him (verse 42) shows that again something important follows. The disciples know, as any Jew would, that the Gentiles have their lordly rulers and great men who revel in their exercise of authority. For the Jew, only God's rule was worthy of such revelry. There is to be a yet different standard among the followers of Jesus; the *great among you* (verse 43) are the servants, and whoever wishes to be at the top must learn to be *slave of all* (verse 44).

There is no more elemental lesson than this in the Gospel of Mark. Servanthood is the essence of discipleship. The model of such discipleship is in the crucified one himself, who also gave *his life as a ransom for many* (verse 45).

The word *ransom* is used in various ways to refer to the redeeming of a slave or a relative, or to payment of the sacrifice required to reclaim a firstborn child from the service of God. It is a metaphor, and speaks about the high and costly price of redemption. Nowhere is there any attempt to say to whom the price was paid.

In the first part of this section, Jesus seems to agree that there are places of preference in the Kingdom, but denies that it is his right to assign them. In the second part, however, he seems to deny that there are any such places, and affirms that all alike are expected to practice servanthood. Mark has probably taken over a piece of tradition in which some disciples have a discussion with Jesus about ranks in the Kingdom, to which Mark has appended his own view regarding what is really important, the concept of servanthood.

The Seeing Blind Bartimaeus (10:46-52)

Verse 46 sets the locale for the final scene in this chapter in Jericho, about fifteen miles from Jerusalem. Probably the story has this association in its pre-Markan form.

Bartimaeus is a *blind beggar* (NRSV) or *blind man* (NIV) (verse 46), the son of Timaeus. He hears of the healer Jesus of Nazareth and cries out, *Jesus, Son of David, have mercy on me!* His only hope has come his way, and he continues to cry for help, even though some *rebuked him* (NIV) or *sternly ordered him* (NRSV) (verse 48). They are only interested in seeing and hearing this notable man who is passing through town.

Bartimaeus' cries are heard by Jesus, who calls for him. Casting aside his outer garment (verse 50) and rushing toward Jesus are signs of a hopeful faith. Jesus' question to Bartimaeus (verse 51) does not mean that Jesus does not know what the man wants; rather, Bartimaeus is given a chance to express his faith. He does so in respectful terms: In the NIV it is translated: *Rabbi, I want to see* and in the NRSV: *My teacher, let me see again* (verse 51).

Little is made of the actual healing. In characteristic fashion the healing is rooted in Bartimaeus' faith (verse 52). And the consequence is that Bartimaeus also joins the ranks of disciples. But nothing is said of the marveling reaction of the bystanders, a customary element in such stories. Evidently Mark wishes to emphasize something else.

In fact Bartimaeus, with his trustful attitude and movement toward faith, stands in sharp contrast to the disciples. They ask about positions of rank and preference in the Kingdom; he only asks for mercy from Jesus. He is blind but sees; they see but are blind.

The Message of Mark 10

The dominant theme in this chapter is discipleship. Along the way to Jerusalem, Jesus attempts to convey to his disciples the high cost of discipleship. He emphasizes that the new community existing in his name operates according to a standard different from the usual reckoning of the world. In Jesus' community there are no places of rank and preference, but all alike are servants.

Wealth and possessions are not guarantees or signs of special favor; they may even get in the way of attaining the Kingdom. And even divorce, practiced everywhere, is not allowed to those who aspire to follow Jesus. As usual, the disciples embody all who simply do not grasp this fundamental point about Jesus and his work.

We can sum up these insights in the following way.

§ Following the crucified one brings with it a cost that not all are prepared to pay, and many do not even understand.

§ In discipleship to Jesus the standards of the world are abandoned; a new standard, the way of servanthood, is taken up as the model of the Kingdom.

§ In this new way of discipleship, something fundamental about the nature of God and the structure of the universe is disclosed. The God who appears in the work and words of Jesus is the servant-God, who gains by giving up and rules by dying.

§ Jesus' glorious rule is not denied, but affirmed only in and through the way of the cross.

§ § § § § § §

Introduction to This Chapter

Jesus comes now to Jerusalem, entering the city to the acclaim of the gathered crowd. The whole scene has overtones of divine determination; Jesus knows his destiny and goes about fulfilling it. The cleansing of the Temple follows, though Mark is careful to separate Jesus from any sort of political activity. The enigmatic fig tree incident brackets the cleansing story, while debate over Jesus' authority, provoked by the cleansing scene, concludes the chapter.

Here is an outline of this chapter.
  I. Jesus' Entrance into the City (11:1-11)
 II. Cursing the Fig Tree (11:12-14)
III. The Cleansing of the Temple (11:15-19)
IV. The Interpretation of the Fig Tree (11:20-26)
 V. The Issue of Jesus' Authority (11:27-33)

Jesus' Entrance into the City (11:1-11)

The entrance scene is set by the geographical note in verse 1. Both villages lie near Jerusalem, though Bethphage is nearer, and the mention of it first is odd. In Zechariah 14:4 the Mount of Olives would be split in two on the Day of the Lord, as God appeared to do battle with the enemies of Israel.

The *village ahead of you* apparently refers to Bethany, where the two unnamed disciples would find a colt tied, on which no one has ever ridden (verse 2). An explanation for this action is not to be found in some prearrangement of Jesus with an otherwise unknown friend in Bethany. Rather, Mark is emphasizing that Jesus is in full command of the situation and knows already what is to transpire. The untrained colt witnesses to the uniqueness of Jesus as Messiah, who rides an animal especially consecrated for him.

The disciples go away and find the colt as Jesus has instructed them, *outside in the street* tied near a door (verse 4). The obscurity of the location only heightens the divine character of the action. The fulfillment motif is pervasive, as Jesus' word comes about in the questioning of the bystanders (verse 5) as to the actions of the disciples. Relating Jesus' word is sufficient for the bystanders to let them go (verse 6).

The colt is brought to Jesus, all in fulfillment of Zechariah 9:9, though only Matthew actually quotes the text (see Matthew 21:5). That the disciples *threw their garments on it* (verse 7) is a gesture of honor in recognition of Jesus' messianic status, as is also a similar act of the crowd in spreading *clothes* (NIV) or *cloaks* (NRSV) on the road (verse 8). Mark does not speak of any palm leaves, which are found only in the Gospel of John (12:13). Rather, Mark says that the crowd *spread leafy* (NIV omits) *branches which they had cut in the fields* (verse 8). The word for *leafy branches* usually describes the mattress stuffing in a bed made of rushes or leaves; in this context it must refer to the same material of which such beds were made. The deed recalls the pilgrim festival of Tabernacles, where the celebrants paraded around the Temple precincts waving branches and singing hymns (the *Hallel*; see Psalm 118).

The crowd surrounds Jesus, so that *those who went ahead and those who followed* shout words of acclamation (verse 9). *Hosanna* is a plea for deliverance; it means something like, "Save us now!" The one *who comes in the name of the Lord* (verse 9) and the *kingdom of our father*

(NIV) or *ancestor* (NRSV) *David* (verse 10) are both slogans expressing Israel's nationalistic hope. *Hosanna in the highest* has a strange sound; it might mean in a broad sense, "To the greatest degree save us now!," or perhaps, "Let the heavens save us now!"

Verse 11 appears to be a Markan editorial conclusion to the scene. Having Jesus make a kind of inspection tour of the Temple in Jerusalem seems superfluous, and neither Matthew nor Luke include it (see Matthew 21:12-17; Luke 19:45-48). Mark has probably inserted this notice here as an introduction to the fig tree incident, which he sandwiches between the entrance into the city and the cleansing of the Temple.

Cursing the Fig Tree (11:12-14)

The following day (verse 12), after a night in Bethany, Jesus returns to Jerusalem and is hungry. He sees a fig tree *in leaf* in the distance (verse 13), that is, it has foliage but no figs yet, which do not appear until early summer. Naturally Jesus finds only leaves, since the crop had not yet appeared. Sounding somewhat petulant, he then utters a curse over the tree (verse 14), which, Mark notes, the disciples hear.

The scene is problematic. We seem to have a picture of a hungry Jesus, disappointed at finding nothing to eat on a tree which is not supposed to be bearing anyway, and cursing the tree so that it withers away. And, furthermore, it seems curious that Jesus would not realize that the tree would have no figs, since figs are not in season. So why is it cursed?

The original Greek also contains an anomaly in verse 14, where the text literally reads, *he said to it [the tree]*, as though something has already been spoken and is now missing. It is also strange that Jesus addresses the tree; the point of that is not merely to utter the curse in the right direction, but to allow the disciples to hear.

The language of the oath is interesting. The word

translated *ever* is literally "into the age." This word often appears in apocalyptic contexts describing the new age. It is also true that some pictures of the new age describe its blessings in terms of overflowing abundance of crops.

If we put these elements together, we might assume that the fig story originally was intended to portray Jesus' disappointment that the new age of the Kingdom had not yet arrived, since the tree lacked the evidence of the abundant crop. But certainly there are problems with even this more imaginative interpretation of the scene. It does not, for example, help us understand why the barren fig tree should be cursed for being barren. Some commentators have suggested that we have here an enacted parable, in which a story by Jesus was turned into a story about Jesus. But what the story was about originally can hardly be determined anymore.

Other commentators find help in Luke 13:6-9, where an unfruitful fig tree appears to be an allegorical symbol for a fruitless Israel. They see in the fig tree in Mark another representation of Israel. The point in the incident originally would then be God's judgment over a fruitless Israel.

Other interpretations are intended to excuse Jesus' seemingly bizarre behavior. However, the story in its entirety communicates a lesson of some sort from Mark the evangelist. It cannot be fully understood without looking at verses 20-26 (see below).

The Cleansing of the Temple (11:15-19)

The phrase *Those who were selling and buying in the temple* describes what sounds like commerce, but refers to the activity generated by the sacrificial system. Suppliers of sacrificial creatures—animals, birds, and so forth—were allowed in the court of the Gentiles for the benefit of worshipers making their offering in the Temple. The law was very explicit about what was acceptable and what was not. Also authorized were the *moneychangers* needed by foreign Jews who had to have local coinage in order to pay the Temple tax.

There may have been abuse—certainly there was potential for it—in these financial arrangements. It seems likely that these activities were controlled by the priesthood, but what disposition was made of the funds is debated among the rabbis. In any case, Mark's purpose was not to present Jesus as a social/religious reformer by the act of driving out these Temple officials. It is probable that Jesus did run out these persons from the Temple, and did so as an act of prophetic symbolism. But Mark gives his own interpretation to the recollection of that deed.

The statement that he *would not allow anyone to carry anything* (NRSV) or *merchandise* (NIV) *through the temple* gives us pause. Does Mark really mean that Jesus was simply irritated by people taking a shortcut through the Temple area? The Greek text says explicitly that no *vessel* was permitted. There is a rabbinic ruling that no staff, or wallet, or sandal, or dust from the feet should be permitted in the Temple.

But Mark seems to have in mind something larger. Permitting no vessel in the Temple would, in effect, shut down the activity of the Temple. Mark may be trying to tell us that the whole sacrificial system came to an end. The appearance of Jesus in Jerusalem, the coming of the crucified one, represents the end of the sacrificial system. Hence the attack on the Temple was not undertaken simply as a reform movement within Judaism, nor as an effort to rouse a rebellion. For Mark this event represents the end of Judaism's worship.

Jesus then taught (verse 17) by alluding to Jeremiah's famous Temple sermon (Jeremiah 7:11). There is deliberate universalism in the assertion that the Temple was intended for *all the nations* (verse 17). Israel's abandonment of its peculiar heritage is shown in its allowing the Temple to become a *den of robbers* (verse 17). That supplies a ground for the claim that now a new way of approaching God, through the ultimate once-for-all sacrifice of the Christ, has come about.

Such a deed would threaten the officials in the Temple, on whose domain Jesus treads severely. It is not surprising that they *began looking for a way to kill him* (verse 18). In this fashion Mark sets up the debates and controversies that follow. At the same time the authorities cannot immediately act against Jesus, because *the whole crowd was amazed* (NIV) or *spellbound* (NRSV) *at his teaching* (verse 18). Jesus and the disciples then leave the city peacefully.

The Interpretation of the Fig Tree (11:20-26)

The setting is the morning of the next day, and the disciples and Jesus pass by the fig tree, now withered away to its roots (verse 20). How they know it has withered all the way to the roots is irrelevant; the emphasis is on the thoroughness of the effect of Jesus' word. Peter's remark is superfluous, and his address to Jesus (*Master*, or literally, *Rabbi*) hardly rises to the occasion. His surprise (*Look!*) is an indirect comment on his faithlessness, since already he knows of Jesus' word addressed to the fig tree.

The lessons to be drawn from the fig tree now follow. This section is probably Mark's own interpretation. Jesus' initial response, *Have faith in God* (verse 22), is the first lesson. The fig tree speaks of what faith can do. The amplifying comment that faith can even move the mountain (verse 23) need not be taken literally. It is hyperbole designed to make its point forcefully.

Verse 24 extends the lesson to the practice of prayer. Asking *in prayer* (verse 24) attaches a more specific condition. The promise is bold: *believe that you have received it, and it will be yours* (verse 24). The saying does not give license to expect just anything, for not everything can in good conscience be asked for in prayer. God is not operating a sugar candy factory, but running a school of discipleship. It would be completely self-contradictory for Mark to emphasize the price of discipleship and then to boldly promise anything a believer asked for.

The traditional words on being prepared to forgive are also attached to this context. The asking-in-prayer is then modified to include the condition that one should always be prepared in his or her praying to *forgive* (verse 25).

How do these lessons relate to the episode on the cursed fig tree? Evidently Mark wants us to see that event as a stimulus to reflect on the possibilities of faith. They are not possibilities without conditions, however, and these somewhat miscellaneous sayings on faith and prayer are intended for the reader to come to that understanding.

The Issue of Jesus' Authority (11:27-33)

After the cleansing of the Temple, an appropriate debate over the authority of Jesus follows. The scene is set again in Jerusalem in the Temple, and this time the chief priests, the scribes, and the elders furnish the opposition (verse 27). The various groups represent the composition of the Sanhedrin, or highest legal body in Judaism. Their question to Jesus (verse 28) has in mind his credentials as a representative from God.

Jesus' response turns the question back to the questioner (verse 29). The questioners become the questioned, and are directed to answer about John the Baptist. The question of whether the baptism of John was from heaven or from humans inquires into the assessment of John's authority. Jesus' own authority is implied in his rather stern, *Answer me* (NRSV) or *tell me* (NIV). Mark explains that the authorities *argued with one another* (NRSV) or *discussed it among themselves* (NIV) (verse 31), since they stand to lose however they respond.

The authorities are faced with a dilemma. Either they affirm John's authority from God and admit their failure to believe him, or they lose standing with the populace who believe that John was indeed a prophet (verse 32). Their silence leads to Jesus' silence. He is not yet prepared to acknowledge his messianic status.

§ § § § § § §

The Message of Mark 11

In this chapter Mark brings Jesus finally to
Jerusalem. The entrance into the city has ironic
overtones, as the assembled crowd shouts at Jesus its
narrowly nationalistic hopes. Jesus is indeed the
coming one, but he does not fulfill the role expected of
him. Instead of leading an army against the Romans, he
enters the city and mounts an assault on the Temple
itself. He then offers lessons in the possibilities of
faith-in-prayer and debates further with the officials of
Judaism. Throughout the chapter the picture of the
surprising Messiah dominates. Jesus never seems quite
to come up to anyone's expectations.

We can set out the following theses from this chapter.

§ What we most seem to hope for from God is an
experience of God's glory; especially we want God to
embody our nationalistic dreams and aspirations, and we
assume that they are God's will for us.

§ The possibilities of faith are limitless, but they occur
in the context of the experience of the crucified Christ.
What is possible for faith has to happen under the sign of
the cross, not apart from it.

§ The authority of Jesus is not evident merely from his
works. No amount of miraculous deeds can demonstrate
who he is, and always there remains a decision to be
made. That decision is the essence of faith itself.

§ § § § § § §

Introduction to This Chapter

The theme of controversy continues. A series of issues comes up, as Jesus confronts the Jerusalem authorities regarding matters of political and theological significance. Loyalty to Rome is raised in the question of payment of taxes to Caesar, theological orthodoxy appears in the debate over the resurrection, and the rabbinic argument over the heart of the law is at stake in the matter of the Great Commandment. The question of the Davidic descent of the messiah and warnings with lessons about hypocrisy and riches conclude the section.

Here follows an outline of this chapter.
  I. The Allegory of the Wicked Tenants (12:1-12)
 II. Concerning Loyalty to Caesar (12:13-17)
III. The Issue of Resurrection (12:18-27)
 IV. The Greatest Commandment (12:28-34)
  V. About the Davidic Messiah (12:35-37)
 VI. Woes Against the Scribes (12:38-40)
VII. The Greatness of the Widow's Gift (12:41-44)

The Allegory of the Wicked Tenants (12:1-12)

Jesus takes up his teaching *in parables* (verse 1). And certainly Jesus did teach in parables, but, as we have seen, a parable for Mark is actually a kind of puzzle to be interpreted allegorically. What follows is, in fact, an allegory that tells the gospel story from the perspective of the post-Easter church of Mark's day.

The setting is reminiscent of Isaiah's song of the vineyard (see Isaiah 5:1-7), and is probably based upon it. The story is about a *man who planted a vineyard* and took great care to see that it yielded a crop, even in the hands of tenants. The situation is that of the absentee landlord, who rents out his land.

At harvest time (verse 2), the landlord sends a servant to collect his due on his vineyard. But the tenants treat the servant badly; they *seized him and beat him, and sent him away empty-handed* (verse 3). A second servant is sent, but he is wounded in the head (verse 4) and dealt with harshly. Still others receive a similar reception: *some they beat and others they killed* (verse 5).

The reception is unbelievably harsh, while the patient endurance of the landlord is incredibly great. Undoubtedly we should see in the servants a disguised reference to the prophets of Israel, while the wicked tenants represent the people of Israel. The point is to say that in its past Israel has continually rejected the messengers of God, even though God has exercised infinite patience with the people.

The sending of the beloved son (verse 6) is a transparent reference to the coming of Jesus. The son's reception is no better, for the tenants took him *and killed him, and threw him out of the vineyard* (verse 8). Obviously the death of Jesus is in view, as the wicked tenants think to rid themselves of the *heir*, so that they might inherit the vineyard.

The owner will come and destroy the tenants, *and give the vineyard to others* (verse 9). Israel will lose its position as the elect people, and that special relationship with God will be given over to others, that is, the church—especially, the church of the Gentiles. The Scripture cited, Psalm 118:22-23 (in the Greek version used in Mark, 117:22-23), is used to confirm the rejection/election theme as *the Lord's doing* (NRSV) or *the Lord has done this* (NIV) (verse 11).

The authorities (*they*, verse 12) then attempt to arrest Jesus, having perceived that they were the ones referred to in the parable (verse 12). They are unable to do so because they feared the crowd, who, Mark seems to say, agreed with Jesus' point of view.

The parable is in reality an allegory reflecting the situation of the Markan church in its debate with Judaism. The debate has actually been settled for Mark, as the allegory makes clear. The position formerly held by Israel has been abandoned in Israel's rejection of its own messiah; now that position has been taken over by the church. The church is now favored by God, and is no longer exclusively Jewish, but is composed of Gentiles as well.

Concerning Loyalty to Caesar (12:13-17)

Verse 13 is another Markan editorial introduction. The *Pharisees* are customary opponents of Jesus, and Mark has probably introduced the *Herodians* here because the issue is political. Their approach is polite, addressing Jesus as *Teacher* (verse 14) and speaking flattering words about Jesus' *true* teaching and his dedication to the way of God. Then they raise their entrapping question: *Is it lawful to pay taxes to Caesar* (NIV) *or the emperor* (NRSV), *or not? Should we pay them, or should we not?* (verse 14).

The question of the lawfulness of taxes exacted by Rome was pertinent to the Jew, for whom only God was the true ruler of Israel. The question has political implications, but also goes to the heart of what it means to be a member of Israel, the people of God.

Jesus knows the *hypocrisy* of his questioners and is not misled by their flattery. That is the thrust of his question, *Why put me to the test?* (NRSV) or *Why are you trying to trap me?* (NIV) (verse 15). The questioners are presented as hypocritical because they are not sincerely seeking an answer, but only trying to entrap Jesus.

Jesus asks for a *coin* (verse 15), literally, a *denarius*, which was about the amount that an ordinary worker might expect to make in a day. His desire to look at it (verse 15) indicates his taking of the initiative in the debate. His question about the inscription on the coin (verse 16) does not mean that he does not possess the information; rather, he is drawing the questioners toward the answer he wishes to give.

When they reply that *Caesar's* (NIV) or *the emperor's* (NRSV) is the image on the coin, then the saying towards which the scene has been leading is delivered: *Give to Caesar the things that are Caesar's, and to God the things that are God's* (verse 17). The scene concludes with a typical reference to the amazement of the questioners.

Much has been written about this saying of Jesus. Some would see here a blueprint for the separation of church and state. Others find that Jesus was actually subordinating the state to the rule of God and, therefore, tacitly endorsing rebellion. In reality, the saying is insufficient in itself to draw such weighty conclusions.

What seems apparent for Mark is that Jesus here disassociates himself from the purely political rebels. What really matters in his calculation is the rule of God. Caesar has his things; the coin bears his image and is rightfully his. But also a new dimension is added to the discussion when *the things that are God's* are entered into the debate. Perhaps there is an implicit contrast between paying what has Caesar's image to Caesar, and paying what has God's image, that is, human beings, back to God. In that case the main point would hinge on giving what human beings owe to God, that is, lives of discipleship.

The Issue of Resurrection (12:18-27)

The *Sadducees* now appropriately furnish the opposition to Jesus, since they are the ones *who say there is no resurrection* (verse 18). And, indeed, the Sadducees were a priestly party, not large numerically but politically powerful, who did not accept new ideas easily.

Since they could not find the concept of resurrection in the Torah or law, they did not believe in it. The concept of resurrection had come into Judaism rather late, and at the time of Jesus was not universally agreed upon.

The Sadducees pose a situation for Jesus that is designed to embarrass anyone believing in resurrection. Just how they knew that Jesus accepted the belief, along with Pharisees and others, the reader is left to guess. The reference to what *Moses wrote* (verse 19) goes back to the levirate law, according to which the brother of a deceased man was expected to take his deceased brother's wife and raise up children for him, so that he did not die without descendants (see Deuteronomy 25:5-10).

The Sadducees then create a hypothetical situation that is logically a *reductio ad absurdam*, that is, a case designed to reduce the opponent's position to absurdity. In the hypothetical case *seven brothers* (verse 20) each in turn play the levirate role and take the wife of a deceased brother. No children are born, *last of all the woman* also died (verse 22). And while the reader of Mark might well wonder about the high risk of marrying this particular woman, the main concern of the situation is to denigrate the idea of resurrection by asking, In *the resurrection whose wife will she be?*

Jesus' response is at first a rebuke (verse 24). The Sadducees misinterpret the Scripture and do not grasp what is possible with God. The real answer is that when they rise from the dead, they neither marry nor are given in marriage, but are like angels in heaven (verse 25). The basic assumption of the question is denied: that the new age will be merely a continuation of the old, with the same rules prevailing. There will not be marriage as usual, for in the transformed state of the new age all will be the same, on the level of the angels in heaven.

Verse 26 then sounds very much like a secondary expansion of the original saying. It refers to the *book of*

Moses, in the passage about the bush (verse 26; see Exodus 3:15), where God is called the *God of Abraham, and the God of Isaac, and the God of Jacob.* The argument is that, since God is God of the patriarchs, they are alive. Therefore, God cannot be *God of the dead, but of the living* (verse 27).

The Greatest Commandment (12:28-34)

A third issue arises from *one of the scribes* (NRSV) or *teachers of the law* (NIV) (verse 28), or experts in the law. He asks a question that was commonly debated among the lawyers, having to do with which commandment was *the most important* (NIV) *first of all* (NRSV). So Jesus is here invoked as authority for the Christian community in this ongoing debate. His answer combines Deuteronomy 6:4-5 and Leviticus 19:18.

The first passage is commonly referred to as the *Shema*, from the Hebrew for the first word in the commandment, meaning *hear*. It speaks of *love* (verse 30) toward God with all one's being. That translates as obedience to God's will. The *second* (verse 31) speaks of duty to the neighbor: *You shall love your neighbor as yourself* (verse 31). Jesus was not the first to combine these two; other examples appear in pre-Christian Judaism, for example, the Testaments of the Twelve Patriarchs. But the important thing is what is meant in this twofold commandment.

Jesus affirms that *there is no other commandment greater than these* (verse 32), and wins the approval of the scribe (verses 32-33), who seems to know well the prophetic tradition. The scribe's comment that the love commandment *is much more important than all (whole* NRSV) *burnt offerings and sacrifices* recalls the critique of the great prophet Amos (see Amos 5:24).

Jesus admires the scribe's wise answer (verse 34), and commends him with, *You are not far from the kingdom of God* (verse 34). The scribe's insight is of the kind that corresponds to the experience of the Kingdom.

Mark concludes this scene, favorable to the scribe, with

the generalizing comment that, due to Jesus' great insight and wisdom, *no one dared to ask him* any more questions (verse 34). Mark means that no hostile questioners reappeared.

This shrinking of the law to the twofold commandment to love God and the neighbor is found throughout the New Testament. The word commonly translated *love* is the word *agape*, which describes that attitude of concern for the other person that does not count on rewards or calculate worth. As directed to God, agape expects obedience to God's will. As directed to the neighbor, agape expects caring that does not notice any differences between one human and another.

About the Davidic Messiah (12:35-37)

Mark has Jesus return to teaching *in the temple* (NRSV) or *temple courts* (NIV) (verse 35). In this instance Jesus inaugurates a discussion with a question about the messiah. He takes up the scribal claim that the *Christ* (NIV) or *Messiah* (NRSV) *is the son of David* (verse 35). According to widespread expectation, the messiah must be descended from the line of David.

However, this assumption is challenged by the argument that David himself, speaking by the Holy Spirit (verse 36)—since Scripture is so inspired—wrote in the Psalms that the messiah was his lord (see Psalm 110:1). Therefore, the messiah can hardly be *his son* (verse 37).

The mode of argumentation is again rabbinic, hinging on slender meanings in the biblical text. We seem to have here a tradition from that part of the early church which had no concern about the Davidic lineage of Jesus.

In the context of Mark's theological interests the text suggests that Jesus has moved on to a higher level of title, such as Son of God. Perhaps this is a hint of rejection of the Davidic messiahship of Jesus, on the ground that it was too politically inflammatory for Mark.

Woes Against the Scribes (12:38-40)

Jesus is still presumably in the Temple carrying on his teaching (verse 38). He now begins to criticize the scribes, rather strangely, after having just met one who was not far from the Kingdom (verse 34). Again we recognize Mark's editorial hand in providing a setting for the sayings to follow.

The *long robes* (NRSV) or *flowing robes* (NIV) (verse 38) were worn by scribes at times of official religious observance. Here the scribes are condemned for wanting to wear them merely for recognition, and *to be greeted* in the market places (verse 38). The desire for the *best seats in the synagogues* and the *places of honor at banquets* (verse 39) is linked with devouring widow's houses (verse 40) and making a show of religious practice. Society then generally valued rank and social standing, as is still widely the case, but such things do not characterize the new community that walks in the way of Jesus.

The Greatness of the Widow's Gift (12:41-44)

The setting is still in the Temple, *opposite the treasury* (NRSV) or *the place where the offerings were put* (NIV) (verse 41), with Jesus seated to observe persons putting money into the treasury. Just what the treasury was is not certain; perhaps it was the trumpet-shaped vessels in the court of the women where offerings might be left.

The scene hinges on the contrast between the *rich people* who put in large amounts (verse 41), which cost them relatively little, and the *poor widow* who put in two *copper coins* (verse 42). The two coins of the widow are the *lepta*, which Mark explains as equivalent to a *quadrans*, or one sixty-fourth of a denarius, an extremely small amount.

That Jesus called his disciples to him (verse 43) is by now a familiar Markan introduction to something important. The *Truly, I tell you* (NRSV) or *I tell you the truth* (NIV) makes the following saying even more impressively significant. What is astonishing is Jesus' assertion that the widow has put in more than anyone else, since she has given everything *all she had to live on* (verse 44).

§ § § § § § §

The Message of Mark 12

Controversy marks this chapter. Jesus is engaged in various debates, which follow logically on the question about his authority. At stake is the truth of the gospel, the question of Jesus' true identity, and even more importantly, his role. Mark wishes to show the reader an edifying picture of Jesus outwitting his opponents in the learned center of Judaism. At the same time the lessons are very real for Mark's church in its historical situation.

The traditions in this chapter lead to the following central themes.

§ There are those who, like historical Israel, have turned away from the gospel. There are consequences of doing so, and each must live with his or her own fate.

§ Christians have a responsibility to Caesar, and what is rightfully his must be paid. At the same time there is another ruler and another rule that also have a claim. This claim is the ultimate one, beside which the ways of Caesar fade and cannot be allowed to take precedence.

§ To believe in the God of the crucified one is, paradoxically, also to believe in the God of unlimited possibilities. This God of the cross is also God of the living, who gives life even to the dead.

§ To accept the burden of discipleship is to render one's will in obedience to God and service to neighbor.

§ The role of servant is not enacted in order to gain the approval of fellow human beings.

§ God is not interested in our being religious, but in our being fully human beings who are turned in servanthood toward the world.

§ The measure of giving is not the amount, but the devotion the gift expresses.

§ § § § § § §

Introduction to This Chapter

This chapter in Mark is often called the *synoptic apocalypse,* or *little apocalypse.* Certainly this section does not, however, resemble the usual apocalypses, such as Daniel or Revelation. It is evident that Mark wishes to address certain issues with regard to expectation of the end of time, since the material consists of sayings of Jesus on a variety of matters relative to that expectation. But we might more accurately say that this chapter really reflects a great deal of the situation of the Markan church awaiting the Parousia. It therefore provides a strong clue to the historical conditions under which the Gospel of Mark was written.

Here is an outline of this chapter.
  I. The Destruction of the Temple (13:1-2)
 II. Warnings Against False Prophets (13:3-8)
III. Expectation of Tribulation (13:9-13)
IV. The Meaning of the Tribulation (13:14-23)
 V. Signs of the Parousia (13:24-31)
VI. Calculating the End Time (13:32-37)

The Destruction of the Temple (13:1-2)
The setting for the apocalyptic instruction is Jesus speaking with his disciples when he comes out of the Temple. An anonymous disciple introduces Jesus' discourse with a remark about the *massive* (NIV) or *large*

121

(NIV) *stones and magnificent* (NIV) or *large* (NRSV) *buildings* of the Temple (verse 1). Certainly Herod's reconstruction of the Temple was impressive, but the main point here is to lead on to the statement of verse 2.

Jesus' response is to predict the destruction of the Temple: *Not one stone will be left on another;* all *will be thrown down.* The Temple was in fact destroyed in the war with Rome in A.D. 70, and it is therefore tempting to suppose that we have here a prediction in view of the actual fact. In that case this saying would constitute a clue to the dating of Mark, putting it right after the destruction of the Temple.

It is not quite that easy, however. This saying lacks the detail of those predictions that show knowledge of the actual facts, such as the Passion predictions, or Luke's amplified version of the same Temple prediction (see Luke 21:6, 20). Then, too, other ancient prophets in Israel's history had issued similar predictions about the Temple (see Jeremiah 7:14), or even about the city of Jerusalem itself (see Micah 3:12). So the prediction may easily go back to Jesus himself.

On the other hand, Mark may be associating the destruction of the Temple in A.D. 70 with the signs of the End. The actual destruction of the Temple would be one of the signs that the eschatological Kingdom is approaching. Or perhaps the situation is actually the reverse, that the sayings which follow are designed to correct the mistaken view that the destruction of the Temple was a sign of the near end. The latter is the more likely. For Mark the Parousia can only occur after certain cosmic events have taken place.

Warnings Against False Prophets (13:3-8)

The apocalyptic discourse is delivered as Jesus sits on the Mount of Olives across from the Temple (verse 3). We noticed earlier that the Mount of Olives has apocalyptic associations, for example, in the prophecy of Zechariah (14:4-11). The disciples asking Jesus to explain something *privately* is common in Mark, though the mention here of *Andrew* last and apart from his brother Peter is a bit unusual. Perhaps his name was a second thought.

Then these disciples (collectively? in unison?) ask the when-question, the one which stirs the imagination of the apocalyptic writer. The *this* (NRSV) or *these things* (NIV) (verse 4) of their question refers back to the prediction of the destruction of the Temple, while the sign when these things are all to be accomplished looks forward to the remainder of the discourse.

Jesus' answer seems at first to be a dodge, in that, instead of answering the question directly, he issues warnings against false prophets. The point of his answer is that certain signs must appear before the Parousia. The many who come in his name and lead many *astray* (NRSV) or *deceive* (NIV) (verse 5) are difficult to identify. The phrase translated *I am he* is literally *I am*, which is often simply a self-predicate of deities or other highly important persons. Perhaps we are hearing the echo of some self-proclaiming group in Mark's church that has pretensions to positions of grandeur in the church. The fact that they issue their statement in Jesus' name certainly indicates that they are members of the Christian community; they are not outsiders.

Furthermore, the assertion that *wars and rumors of wars* (verse 7) are to be taken as a sign of the impending Parousia is here denied (this must take place, *but the end is still to come*). Similarly, *earthquakes* and *famines* (verse 8) are common elements in apocalyptic schemes as aspects of the End. The true interpretation of such things is that they are *the beginning of the birth-pangs* (NRSV) or *birth-pains* (NIV) (verse 8), that is, the time of tribulation which must come upon the earth before the End. They are not the End itself. The word translated *birth-pangs* or *pains* is a technical term for the period of messianic woes that was thought to precede the coming of the messiah.

Expectation of Tribulation (13:9-13)

Part of the period of eschatological tribulation is the suffering of the faithful. The Christian community is warned to expect hard times. *They* (NRSV—the NIV translates as the *local councils*) is a reference to the authorities, perhaps both synagogue and civil. It is clear that there remains hostility between the Markan church and the synagogue; there is also a threat from the civil authorities (the *governors and kings*).

Being *flogged* (NIV) or *beaten* (NRSV) *in synagogues* (verse 9) is based upon Deuteronomy 25:1-3, and recalls similar punishments endured by the apostle Paul (see 2 Corinthians 11:24-25). All cases are opportunities for the faithful to witness to *them*. The suffering itself witnesses to the gospel of the suffering and crucified one.

The insertion of the condition that *the gospel* (NIV) or *good news* (NRSV) *must first be preached to all nations* sounds like a Markan qualification. Before the End can come the gospel has first to be proclaimed around the world. The intention of the verse is to discourage a too fervent attachment to the "signs" that point to the supposedly imminent End. First there is a universal task.

Essential to that task is the witnessing function. Hence there follow some words of advice on the proper behavior when they bring you to trial (verse 11). To *hand over* (NRSV) or (verse 11) or *arrest* (NIV) is the same word used of Jesus' own passion; its usage here means that the Christian's "passion" is modeled after that of Jesus. Jesus has his passion, and so likewise does his disciple.

Like Jesus, disciples are not to be anxious about what they are to say (verse 11), for they will have the presence of the Holy Spirit. The words of the faithful are as the words of the Spirit. So few are the references to the Spirit in Mark that little can be deduced as to what was Mark's concept. Here it can at least be said that the Spirit acts for the believer and is therefore an intercessor. Whether Mark thought of the Spirit as the same as the risen Lord (see 2 Corinthians 3:17) is less clear.

Conflict within families is a reality in the Markan church, and such things happened in the Christian mission. Allegiance to the gospel was divisive, as brother was set against brother, father against child, and children against their parents (verse 12). This is not a pretty picture; it is intended to present squarely the high cost of following the crucified one. Indeed, you will be hated by all because of me (verse 13). The *you* is plural; all Christians face the possibility. *All* refers to the society generally.

Here is the image of an apocalyptic community faced with a hostile world, turning into itself for consolation and turning outward to continue its imperative mission. The promise that whoever endures to the end will be saved provides a ground of hope to the sufferers. Before them lies the eschatological Kingdom. There are the ingredients of martyrdom here. But Mark's focus on the suffering of the believer does not arise from a desire for a martyr's death, but rather from the model provided by the ransoming deed of the crucified one.

The Meaning of the Tribulation (13:14-23)

The whole of this apocalypse has been much influenced by Old Testament language and imagery. The Book of Daniel was one important source; it was probably even in the stage of development before Mark. So the reference to the *abomination that causes desolation* (NIV) or *desolating sacrilege* (NRSV) (verse 14) evokes Daniel 9:27; see also 11:31; 12:11. There the sacrilege referred originally to the act of Antiochus Epiphanes, Seleucid king of Syria, in setting up a pagan altar in the Temple in Jerusalem. His deed was part of a larger campaign to destroy the Jewish religion, and precipitated the Maccabean Revolt in 165 B.C.

This metaphor has obviously shifted ground and has some other value in Mark. That it remains somewhat mysterious is emphasized in the admonition to *let the reader understand* (verse 14). One possibility for interpreting the reference to the desolating sacrilege is to see in it the action of the mad emperor Caligula, who in A.D. 41 attempted to have his image set up in the Temple in Jerusalem. That act nearly provoked a revolt among the Jews and was doubtless seen in apocalyptic circles as a sign of the tribulation accompanying the End. Fortunately, Caligula did not stay alive long enough to carry out his policies.

The sacrilege reference also could have in mind the destruction of the Temple in A.D. 70, in Mark's own day. However, the depiction of the sacrilege as being set up does not quite agree with that interpretation. What we seem to have here in this section from verse 14 through verse 23 is a pre-Markan apocalypse that apparently grew out of the Judean church. Mark the evangelist found it useful because of its vivid characterization of the woes of the tribulation period, and included it in his apocalyptic section. We need to exercise some care, therefore, in relating everything in these verses to Mark's own situation.

This desolating sacrilege is a sign for those who are living in Judea to *flee to the mountains* (verse 14). The reference to Judea makes it plain that the prophetic warnings here originated in a Palestinian church. The urgency of flight is emphasized in the further admonition not to descend from the housetop to enter the house to carry away goods (verse 15). The picture is that of the flat roof in Palestine where homeowners often went at night to cool off or to sleep. There will be no time for such considerations. Similarly, the farmer out in the field (verse 16) need not bother to return for his mantle, or outer garment, which he laid aside while he worked in the field.

Just why the eschatological moment is especially hard on those who are with child or those who are nursing children (verse 17) is not quite clear. The thought is apparently that bearing and raising children show confidence that the future will continue like the past, whereas in fact the last time is at hand.

The caution to Pray that it may not happen in winter (verse 18) means that conditions of cold would only further intensify the misery of the tribulation. This tribulation will exceed anything the world has witnessed since the beginning, or can ever expect (verse 19). The term *distress* (NIV) or *suffering* (NRSV) is a technical one often appearing in apocalyptic contexts to refer just to this terrible time right before the End itself.

The mercy of the Lord (verse 20) in shortening this time of tribulation is a theme which also appears with some regularity in apocalyptic writings. This time period appears in Daniel as three and one-half years, a length of time also mentioned in the Book of Revelation. It is only *for the sake of the elect* that the time is not longer. The theme of God's mercy toward the elect, or the chosen, is also attested in apocalyptic writings of that era. Mark no doubt wants us to think of the elect as the church.

Verses 21-22 then seem to return to the theme with which Mark began, the idea that false prophets will appear. The onset of tribulation does not mean that the Parousia is imminent (verse 21). *False Christs* (NIV) or *messiahs* (NRSV) and false prophets are to be expected in the period of tribulation. They will attempt to lead astray the faithful with *signs and miracles* (NIV) *omens* (NRSV) (verse 22), that is, claims of miracle-working ability.

Possibly we are listening in here on the claims of some self-inflating group in the Markan church which put itself out as the very incarnation of Jesus himself, or at least as his authorized prophets. They must have laid claim to special powers and proclaimed the imminence of the End in their own works. Mark intends for the reader to be aware of the possibility of deception by such leaders (verse 23).

Signs of the Parousia (13:24-31)

Mark now sets forth the true vision of the Parousia. It is in those days, after that suffering (verse 24) that one might expect to see the Parousia, and only when preceded by certain cosmic events. (See verses 24-25.) In other words, there will be unmistakable signs in the heavens before the Parousia occurs. Such imagery is familiar also in apocalyptic works of the time. These supernatural portents mean that some special action of God is at hand.

It is then that they *will see the Son of man coming in clouds with great power and glory* (verse 26). Again the *they* is a generalization meaning "everyone" or "all people at that time." The *clouds* recall the Old Testament imagery of the *shekinah* or tabernacle as a symbol for the presence of the divine. The *power and glory* contrast with the picture of the present, lowly Christ. There is a proper hope of glory in Mark, but it is never to be separated from the way of the crucified one.

The sending out of the angels to *gather his elect from the four winds*, which is further defined as *the ends of the earth to the ends of heaven* (verse 27), is often called "the rapture" today. That terminology is not taken from the New Testament; the idea, however, is that at the Parousia Christ will claim his own. The role of the angels in the last days is attested in other apocalyptic writings.

This promise of vindication in the last days was very powerful to the Markan church, faced as it was with adversity. Yet at the same time this hope was not allowed to override everything else, so that the Christians of Mark's day merely sat back to await their reward. That would have been a misunderstanding. There are discipleship and mission in the present, grounded in, but not submerged under, the hope of the future.

Verses 28-31 then undergird this promise, in a somewhat miscellaneous grouping of sayings. First is a lesson to be learned from the fig tree (verse 28). Anyone would know that the appearance of the bud means that *summer is near*. The lesson is that when the fig tree blossoms, they will realize that Jesus is near, *at the very gates* (NRSV) or *right at the door* (NIV) (verse 29). The cosmic events are the determining sign that the Parousia is at hand. The *gates* or *door* is an image drawn from city life; it means that the Son of man is standing at the entrance to the city, prepared to enter.

The explicit promise is then made that *this generation will not pass away until all these things* have happened (verse 30). There is hardly any doubt that *these things* refers to the whole series of events just described, from tribulation to Parousia. The reader of Mark would understand that he or she was standing somewhere near the Parousia.

Whether we take this promise as originating with Jesus himself or coming out of the situation of the Markan church, the promise was not literally fulfilled. *This generation* did not see the Parousia, and no generation has yet seen it. Nevertheless, the hope still remains for the establishment of the ultimate rule of God over the earth.

Calculating the End Time (13:32-37)

In order not to generate enthusiasm for this apocalyptic expectation, it is necessary to add the warning that appears in verse 32. It is striking that here Jesus is denied knowledge of the time of the Parousia. No stronger warning against calculating the time of the Parousia could be issued. If Jesus does not know, then no human authority has even the remotest idea.

In case the lesson is missed, the further admonition is added to keep *alert* (verse 33). A tiny parable gives an illustration of the man going on a journey (verse 34). He leaves his servants with tasks to do, and expects the doorkeeper to be ready to open the door for him. That is exactly the situation of the church as it awaits the Parousia.

What is important is not to know the exact moment, but to *watch* (NIV) or *keep awake* (NRSV) (verse 35), since no one knows even the time of day for the Parousia. Worst of all would be to be found *asleep* (verse 36), not literally, but spiritually, and therefore unprepared. Accordingly, the last word must be: *watch* (NIV) or *keep awake* (NRSV) (verse 37).

§ § § § § § §

The Message of Mark 13

In this chapter issues relating to the hope of the ultimate rule of God through Christ have been exposed. The picture is drawn very deliberately by Mark, with appropriate emphasis upon the certainty of that rule that must finally prevail, but also on the reserve expected of faith in seeking out the time of the End. To be sure, there are signs for those who have the eyes to see. The faithful can expect to pass through hard times; false leaders will arise to deceive. And at the Parousia there will be no uncertainty; the appearance of Christ in his eschatological role will be unmistakable. Meanwhile, the task of the faithful community is to proclaim the gospel throughout the world, and to conduct its mission with patience and watchfulness.

We may summarize these themes in the following way.

§ However it may appear that history is going, however much it may seem that history is gaining the upper hand, it remains the object of Christian hope that God's rule will triumph.

§ The community of faith needs to have eyes to perceive false messiahs and false prophets; they are those who betray its hope and proclaim victory where there is still to be trod the way of the cross.

§ Speculating over the time of the Parousia is not an appropriate activity for faith; only God knows, and will bestow this knowledge at the right time.

§ § § § § § §

Introduction to This Chapter

The Passion narrative is introduced by the story of the anointing of Jesus; the familiar themes of the betrayal, the Supper, and the arrest in Gethsemane follow. The disciples' final failure is embodied in their desertion in Gethsemane and especially in Peter's dramatic denial of Jesus. Before that, the trial of Jesus by the Sanhedrin gives opportunity for Mark to set out plainly Jesus' claim to messiahship and the basis for his condemnation. Throughout the section the focus is upon the meaning of Jesus and his work in the world.

Here follows an outline of this chapter.
   I. The Anointing of Jesus' Body (14:1-9)
  II. Judas's Intention to Betray Jesus (14:10-11)
 III. Preparation for the Supper (14:12-16)
  IV. The Last Supper (14:17-25)
   V. Struggle in Gethsemane (14:26-42)
  VI. Jesus' Arrest in the Garden (14:43-52)
 VII. Jesus Before the Sanhedrin (14:53-65)
VIII. Peter's Denial (14:66-72)

The Anointing of Jesus' Body (14:1-9)
The story begins with the note that it was two days before the Passover and the feast of Unleavened Bread (verse 1). The feast of Unleavened Bread began on the same day as Passover and ran for a week. Both feasts celebrated the Exodus from Egypt.

Normally Passover was marked by a ritual meal held on the evening of 15 Nisan (roughly March-April of our calendar). Mark has the crucifixion occur on the day of that same evening, on Friday. He therefore seems to put the conspiracy to kill Jesus on Wednesday. However, he explicitly says that the meal was on Thursday, on Passover itself (14:12). This problem in chronology points to the fact that an older version underlies Mark's story which has not been completely integrated with Mark's point of view.

Mark depicts a conspiracy of the *chief priests and the scribes* (NRSV) or *teachers of the law* (NIV) to rid themselves of Jesus. The Romans are not involved here, nor is there any hint of an official Sanhedrin action.

The intention of the authorities not to arrest Jesus *during the feast* (NIV) or *festival* (NRSV) (verse 2) was not actually carried out, if we follow Mark's chronology. In fact, as Mark portrays it, Jesus was arrested right after the Passover meal, and was tried and executed during Passover itself.

The story of Jesus' anointing is set in *Bethany*, where Jesus is staying in the house of an otherwise unknown *Simon the leper* (verse 3), who was presumably healed by Jesus.

An *alabastar jar* was a vessel with a long neck, which was broken off when the contents were used. *Nard* was a perfume extracted from the root of a rare plant from India, and therefore very expensive. Thus some who are present complain that the perfume or ointment was wasted (verse 4), since its value was above 300 denarii, or almost what an average worker could make in a year.

Their reproach is that so much could have been given to the poor (verse 5). We might have expected Jesus to agree. But instead he pronounces a blessing over the anonymous woman. And the ground of his blessing is that, while you always have the poor with you (verse 7), and you ought to do for them as much as possible, nevertheless *you will not always have me* (verse 7). Therefore, the woman has done a good deed in anointing the body of Jesus beforehand for burial (verse 8). The saying presupposes the Jewish custom of anointing the dead with spices and oil. There was no practice of embalming.

The woman's deed will be remembered wherever the good news is preached in the whole world (verse 9). The weight of this promise is accented by the stereotyped phrase, *truly, I tell you*, or *I tell you the truth* (NIV) literally, Amen, I tell you. The Amen at the beginning instead of the end was characteristic for Jesus, and meant that what followed was of great significance, to be heard with special care.

Judas's Intention to Betray Jesus (14:10-11)

Judas goes to the *chief priests in order to betray* him to them (verse 10). The word rendered *betray* is the same as in the Passion predictions, meaning to *hand over*, or *deliver up*. The betrayal of Jesus was a handing over or delivering up to the forces of evil, which did with him as they pleased. And yet, paradoxically, it all occurred within the will of God.

What Judas did or why he did it is not clear. Mark suggests that the authorities *promised to give him money* (verse 11), but they did so only after Judas came to them voluntarily.

Preparation for the Supper (14:12-16)

The time for the Last Supper is the first day of Unleavened Bread, when they sacrificed the passover lamb (verse 12). Mark presents the Last Supper as occurring on Passover, but there are problems with the chronology. The sacrifice of the paschal lambs occurred on the day before Passover (14 Nisan), not the first day of the feast.

What Mark wishes to emphasize in including this set of instructions for carrying out the supper is that Jesus fully commands the situation. Thus Jesus *sent two of his disciples* (verse 13) into the city (Jerusalem) where they would encounter *a man carrying a jar of water*. He would point out the place where the supper was to be held. Even the words to be spoken to the *owner of the house* (verse 14) are given. All this happens by divine determination, even having a *large upper room furnished and ready* (verse 16).

The Last Supper (14:17-25)

Jesus came *with the twelve* (verse 17) at the evening of Passover. That would have been after sunset the night of 15 Nisan. While they are eating Jesus announces his betrayer, someone *who is eating* (NIV) or *dipping bread into the bowl* (NRSV) *with me* (verse 18). Sharing of table fellowship indicated acceptance and intimacy among friends. It is all the more ironic that betrayal occurs in that setting.

The disciples question who is involved (verse 19), and Jesus' answer points unequivocally to Judas: *It is one of the twelve* (verse 20), he says, the same one who is at the moment sharing a dish with him. There is a deliberate echo here of Psalm 41:9, which calls the attention of the reader to the divine ordering of the entire story.

Great irony is expressed in the saying about the *Son of man* who goes *as it is written of him* (verse 21). If this Son of man has to go the way of the cross, how then is Judas to be blamed? This paradox is never resolved. Both human freedom and God's determination are held with equal vigor. Consequently, *woe* falls upon the betrayer, who would have been better off if he had not been born (verse 21), though Mark does not report the fate of Judas.

Then Jesus acts sacramentally: *he took bread, gave thanks, and broke it, and gave it to his disciples saying, "Take it; this is my body"* The NRSV revises it: *he took a loaf of bread, and after blessing it he broke it, gave it to them, and said, "Take; this is my body."* (verse 22). The language doubtless reflects the actual practice in the Markan community. The blessing of the bread was customary before meals. The word for bread describes ordinary cakes of bread, not unleavened bread, as might be expected if the meal were originally a Passover observance. The drinking of the cup after having given *thanks* (verse 23) communicated to the faithful that they were included in the *covenant which is poured out for many* and which was made possible by Jesus' self-giving.

The idea of the new covenant was based upon the prophecy in Jeremiah 31:31-34. It affirms that Jesus' sacrifice provided the basis for a new relationship with God, no longer based upon the law.

The final saying in the scene offers a clue to another interpretation of the Last Supper. Here there is no Passover allusion in the promise that I will not drink again *of the fruit of the vine until that day when I drink it new in the kingdom of God* (verse 25). The implication is of an age in decline; the Kingdom draws near, and there is to be no more celebrating until it is manifest. Indeed, it seems likely that the Last Supper was originally some sort of eschatological celebration, anticipating the coming kingdom of God. This originally eschatological saying was no doubt seen by Mark as a prophetic statement on Jesus' part, anticipating his ransoming death *for many* (verse 24).

Struggle in Gethsemane (14:26-42)

The singing of a *hymn* was typical at the conclusion of a Passover. On the *Mount of Olives* (verse 26), Jesus' prediction of the flight of the disciples shows his foreknowledge of events. That the disciples will *fall away* (NIV) or *become deserters* (NRSV) (verse 27) is seen already in Scripture (Zechariah 13:7). The Zechariah text functions allegorically: the *I* is God, Jesus is the shepherd, and the disciples are the sheep.

Verse 28 anticipates the words of the angel at the empty tomb (16:7). It is intended to give assurance even in the face of the disciples' failure. Verse 29 then seems to ignore this promise, with *Peter* loudly proclaiming his loyalty to the death. Jesus responds with the prediction of Peter's denial. The crowing of the cock *twice* normally would signify the end of the night. Peter protests *vehemently* (NRSV) or *empathically* (NIV) (verse 31) that, under threat of death, he *will not deny* (NRSV) or *disown* (NIV) Jesus. To *deny* has a legal connotation, and suggests total disavowal before a judge. It is often connected with eschatological confirmation of a relationship with Jesus.

The disciples all *said the same* as Peter. Here again Mark's sense of irony is at work, for the most conspicuous thing about the disciples was their utter failure at Jesus' crucial hour.

In *Gethsemane* Jesus goes apart with the usual three inner disciples to *pray* (verse 32). In his distress (verse 33) he struggles with God, asking of his disciples that they remain here and watch (verse 34), that is, not stand guard looking for enemies, but stay with Jesus in his agony.

Jesus prostrates himself, in the mode of supplication to God, flat on the ground (verse 35). His prayer is for deliverance from his terrible destiny, if it were *possible* (verse 35). The conditional clause in Greek means that it is possible, but whether it may be done has yet to be decided.

Jesus expresses that thought in his address (verse 36). The unique word *Abba* is an Aramaic term which really means something like "Daddy," and was the way a very little child spoke to his or her father. Jesus taught his disciples to use this word to address God, as if to say that we are all like little children before God, and can only speak haltingly to and of God.

Jesus then finds his disciples sleeping while he was struggling. He rebukes them (verse 37) and warns them against entering *into temptation* (NIV) or *time of trial* (NRSV) (verse 38), adding the terse comment that *the spirit (indeed) is willing, but the flesh* (NRSV) or *body* (NIV) *is weak* (verse 38). The word rendered *temptation* (NIV) or *time after* (NRSV) means *testing*, and refers to the time of eschatological tribulation.

Jesus again goes away to his private agony, and returns to the disciples a second and third time to rebuke them for *sleeping* (verses 40-41). With intense irony Mark is shaping his picture of the abject failure of the disciples.

Abruptly Jesus announces that It is *enough* (verse 41). The single word in Greek is hard to translate; perhaps it means, given the commercial use of the term in Greek, *paid in full*, that is, my account is (about to be) paid up, since *the hour has come*. It is a time of reckoning, for the betrayer is at hand.

Jesus' Arrest in the Garden (14:43-52)

Judas comes along leading a crowd *with swords and clubs* (verse 43). The crowd comes from the chief priests and the scribes and the elders, the Jewish authorities, but the action resembles more a mob action than an official arrest. Such a "popular" gathering against Jesus is hard to reconcile with the earlier notices of his widespread acceptance with the people.

The question of what Judas betrayed arises again at this point. Mark seems to have him merely identifying Jesus with a *kiss* (verses 44-45). The kiss was a sign of affection and honor between teachers and their students.

Jesus is seized after the identifying kiss (verse 46), and an unknown person (disciple?) *drew his sword* (verse 47), and attacks the *slave* (NRSV) or *servant* (NIV) *of the high priest cutting off his ear* (verse 47). Jesus does not rebuke this action (as in Luke 22:51; see also John 18:11), but instead accuses his arresters of treating him like a common criminal. The fact is that he was with them openly every day in the Temple.

The *scriptures* (verse 49) tell the Passion story in advance, though no particular text is cited. The Old Testament was the indispensable source in the early church for understanding the passion of Jesus.

The final failure of the disciples is simply described by Mark: Then everyone *deserted him and fled* (verse 50). Misunderstanding has now become active cowardice.

The curious note about *a young man* (verse 51) who, losing his garment when he was seized, ran off *naked*, may point to an eyewitness to the events. But it is more likely that Mark is exercising his sense of irony again:

The naked youth is like the disciples who, in their flight, are finally also "exposed" for what they truly are.

Jesus Before the Sanhedrin (14:53-65)

The same group of *chief priests and the elders and the teachers of the law* (NIV) or *scribes* (NRSV) mentioned at the arrest of Jesus gather at the home of the *high priest* (verse 53). A meeting of the *whole council* (NRSV) or *Sanhedrin* (NIV) (verse 55) is depicted. But first Mark inserts mention of *Peter* in the *courtyard of the high priest* (verse 54) in order to prepare for the scene of Peter's denial.

The Sanhedrin was the highest legal body in Judaism. There is debate over the extent of its authority, especially whether it had the power of capital punishment, and the historical records are not clear.

Verses 55-59 portray a Sanhedrin acting illegally, even contrary to its own procedure. The authorities seek to find a basis for condemning Jesus to death (verse 55), and bring false testimony against him (verse 56). These witnesses accuse him of threatening the Temple (verse 58), though Mark casually remarks that even so *their testimony did not agree* (verse 59). It is clearly a kangaroo court, and the account is meant to impress upon the reader the absolute innocence of Jesus. The accounts of the trial emanated from a time of extreme hostility between church and synagogue.

A solemn scene follows, as the *high priest stood up before them* (verse 60) to question Jesus. Fulfilling the role of the suffering servant (see Isaiah 53), Jesus was silent and gave no answer (verse 61). But in response to the messianic question (verse 61) Jesus is surprisingly bold: *I am* (verse 62), he says, and goes on to proclaim the expected Parousia. He will shortly be sitting *at the right hand of the Power*, (NRSV) or *Mighty One* (NIV) that is, exalted to God, and then *you* (plural) will see his Parousia (*coming on the clouds of heaven*).

For the first time the secrecy veil is drawn back. Jesus openly acknowledges his messiahship, but only before the Jewish authorities. Mark is saying that the issue with

Judaism is a religious one, centering on the question of who Jesus is. The answer is given supremely in the crucifixion-Resurrection.

That the *high priest tore his clothes* (verse 63)—a sign of consternation—and termed Jesus' statement *blasphemy* demonstrates the true issue between Jews and the Christians of Mark's community. The Christians proclaimed Jesus as God's son and affirmed his deity. To the strictly monotheistic Jews such a claim was bound to be regarded as blasphemous because it usurped the deity of God.

The council agrees with the high priest and *condemned him as deserving* (NRSV) or *worthy of* (NIV) *death* (verse 64). Blasphemy in the sense of explicit cursing of God was punishable by death.

The further maltreatment of Jesus (verse 65) would have been illegal; it is more in keeping with the picture of the servant in Isaiah 53 than with actual circumstances. The command, *Prophesy!* suggests that Jesus was in fact regarded as a prophet leading one of those strange uprisings described by Josephus or mentioned in Acts 5:36-37; 21:38.

Peter's Denial (14:66-72)

Peter is confronted by *one of the servant girls of the high priest* (verse 66), a household servant. She notes to the bystanders (verse 69) that Peter was a companion of the *Nazarene, Jesus* (verse 67), but, moving away (verse 68), Peter denies it. The maid is insistent (verse 69), and Peter is equally vigorous in his denial (verse 70), pretending to be merely one of the crowd. But the crowd, ironically, disowns him, recognizing his speech as Galilean (verse 70). Peter's denial grows more fierce, and he began to invoke curses on himself and to swear (verse 71). Then the *cock crowed for a second time* (verse 72), though the reference to the first time (verse 68) is textually uncertain. When Peter remembers Jesus' word he *broke down and wept* (verse 72).

The story serves Mark's purpose. Now the failure of the disciples is complete; even Peter, the most inner of the inner group, has abandoned Jesus. The story of the disciples is a movement from dullness to denial.

§ § § § § § §

The Message of Mark 14

This chapter is deep in theological material. The anointing, the betrayal, the Last Supper, the arrest and appearance before the Sanhedrin, and Peter's denial, all are familiar themes, yet pregnant with meanings that lie at the core of Christian faith. Let us try to summarize some of the leading themes of this chapter.

§ Devotion to Jesus has its proper place, and expresses gratitude for his passion as a work done "for many."

§ The betrayal of Jesus by Judas remains a mystery to faith. Yet we should realize that the other disciples really did not fare a great deal better. Judas's story confronts every Christian with the question as to whether he or she could have persisted in the face of the Passion.

§ The sacrament represents Jesus in his passion. Through the elements we are participants in his passion and see ourselves included in the community of the new covenant. This experience occurs in the context of hope for the eschatological rule of God.

§ The suffering of Jesus models the suffering which may well come to any disciple. There is no easy path through the cross.

§ Suffering makes clear the reality of Jesus' humanity. It also defines the humanity of disciples.

§ The trial of Jesus expresses paradoxes. While he was in the hands of human authorities, in another sense he was beyond their reach. For even though they condemned him, his death ultimately condemned them.

§ The denial of Peter suggests that the desire to save ourselves reaches the deepest parts of our selfhood. Peter faced losing his life while trying to save it, as did all the disciples. Somehow they got the lesson backwards.

§ § § § § § §

Introduction to This Chapter

The Passion narrative continues. Jesus is brought before Pilate for trial. After examination Pilate relents, under Jewish pressure, and condemns Jesus. The crucifixion follows. The scene at the cross shows compellingly the terrible anguish of Jesus. He dies uttering an agonizing cry. Certain women are introduced who will appear in the empty tomb story. The body is taken by Joseph of Arimathea and buried. All is darkness, leading to the finale in Chapter 16.

Here is an outline of this chapter.
I. Jesus' Trial Before Pilate (15:1-15)
II. The Abuse of Jesus (15:16-20)
III. The Scene of Crucifixion (15:21-39)
IV. The Burial of Jesus (15:40-47)

Jesus' Trial Before Pilate (15:1-15)

Jesus is now taken before Pilate early in the morning (15:1), following a consultation. The term *handed him over* is a technical one in the Passion narrative.

Judea was ruled almost entirely by procurators from 6 to 66. Pontius Pilate exercised the office between A.D. 26 and 36. From other sources we know that he was not a charitable governor, but pursued a policy of toughness toward the Jews and often produced great offense by his actions. The Gospels treat him with kindness, but we should remember that they were composed at a time when it was increasingly important for the church to get along with the empire.

Pilate surprisingly gets to the heart of the matter by asking whether Jesus is *the King of the Jews* (verse 2). The question has political overtones and is the kind of thing in which Rome would have taken great interest. Jesus' reply is noncommittal: You have said so. Mark deliberately stakes out a contrast in Jesus' answers to the Sanhedrin and to Pilate. Before the religious authority, the question is messianic and is answered forthrightly and positively. Before the political authority Jesus hedges. That means: Yes, Jesus is the King of the Jews, but not simply in the political sense.

The Jewish authorities make unspecified charges against Jesus, and Pilate seeks from him an answer to the charges (verse 4). But Jesus made no further answer (verse 5), appropriate to his role as the suffering servant (Isaiah 53). Pilate's wondering is not a step toward faith, but indicates his puzzlement at the mystery of the person before him.

The practice of releasing *a prisoner* (verse 6) in observance of Passover is otherwise unknown to us. *Barabbas* (meaning *Son of Abbas*), a well known rebel who had committed murder during insurrection (verse 7), sounds like a Zealot-type of insurgent, who was caught by the Romans and was awaiting his own fate. We know nothing of the insurrection mentioned here by Mark, though Josephus witnesses to a variety of such events at that time.

The *crowd* (verse 8) now mysteriously appears, demanding the condemnation of Jesus and the release of Barabbas. Mark explains that the crowd is *stirred up* (verse 11) by the chief priests; otherwise, it is impossible to imagine Jesus as the victim of a popular action, when all along he has been portrayed as the hero of the people. Pilate responds in an uncharacteristic way by asking the opinion of the crowd (verse 9). He is made to say that the

Jewish authorities are acting *out of envy* (NIV) (verse 10), that is, motivated by jealousy (NRSV) of Jesus' popularity. Indirectly, of course, to respond positively to people who are motivated thus makes Pilate out to be rather a weak character.

The crowd insists on having Barabbas instead of Jesus (verse 11). Pilate asks the perennial question with regard to Jesus, "What shall I do, *then* with the *one* you call the King of the Jews?" (verse 12). Notice also that Pilate ironically attributes the title of *king* to *you* (plural), the Jews (though some old manuscripts omit the phrase, *you call*).

The crowd becomes an angry mob and cries out for Jesus' death (verse 13). Pilate continues to behave as a model of moderation, asking *Why, what evil* (NRSV) or *crime* (NIV) has he done? (verse 14). Yet he allows himself to be stampeded: *wishing to satisfy the crowd* (verse 15) he gives orders to release Barabbas and have Jesus *scourged* and then *crucified* (verse 15). Scourging or flogging was inflicted on the condemned right before crucifixion.

Mark treats Pilate graciously and puts all the blame on the Jews, especially the officialdom in Judaism. This picture is much influenced by events in the post-Easter period, when church and synagogue had bitter relationships.

The one unavoidable fact is that Jesus was condemned in a Roman court and executed in the Roman manner. Death by crucifixion was Roman practice, imposed upon slaves and revolutionaries. It is obvious that Jesus was not a slave, so clearly he was finally sent to the cross under charges of having violated the *Pax Romana*, or peace of Rome. In other words, he died under charges of attempting to subvert the state.

Mark's sense of irony is also again at work in the Barabbas incident. The point here is that the guilty go free, while the innocent are condemned. Yet it is in this "injustice" of God that redemption becomes a possibility.

The Abuse of Jesus (15:16-20)

The *palace* (verse 16) where Jesus is now taken seems to refer to Herod the Great's Jerusalem headquarters. The explanatory comment equating this place with the *praetorium* sounds strange; perhaps Mark thinks it more understandable to his readers to use a Roman term. The governor's headquarters actually were at Caesarea, where indeed his residence was known as a *praetorium*.

The whole company (verse 16) is summoned to witness the mistreatment of Jesus. The reference is to the *cohort* (NRSV) or *company* (NIV), the tenth part of a legion, or usually about 600 men. It is quite a crowd to observe the punishment of a mere Galilean revolutionary.

The clothing of Jesus *in a purple cloak* (NRSV) or *robe* (NIV) along with twisting a crown of thorns (verse 17) for his head relates to the accusation of political kingship against him. Purple stood for royalty; the crown of thorns is a mocking imitation of the laurel wreath which the Caesars are often shown wearing.

The treatment becomes more violent. The *reed* (NRSV) (verse 19) with which Jesus is struck probably is meant to represent the *staff* (NIV) which rulers sometimes held in hand. Spitting on someone was an act of insult, while kneeling down *in homage to him* (verse 19) is mock imitation of the worship increasingly paid to the emperors. After the mocking Jesus has *his own clothes* (verse 20) returned to him and he is taken away to be crucified.

The Scene of Crucifixion (15:21-39)

Cyrene was in North Africa. Nothing is known of *Simon*, but he would be recognized in the Markan church, since he was the *father of Alexander and Rufus* (verse 21). Paul mentions a Rufus in Romans 16:13, whom he calls *eminent in the Lord*. Simon is conscripted to carry the crossbeam, which the prisoner was customarily made to bear to the site of execution. The upright part would already be there, fixed in the ground.

Golgotha (verse 22) is a transliteration of the Aramaic term *gulgoltah*, which means *skull*. The location is uncertain. Normally the Romans chose conspicuous places, such as the main entrance to a city, so that passersby would not miss the lesson.

The Talmud records that women from Jerusalem provided a narcotic to condemned men, as an act of charity. But the *wine mixed with myrrh* (verse 23) offered to Jesus would have been a modest pain killer. Myrrh was an aromatic gum used in a variety of ways, including preparation of corpses. Perhaps Mark is again writing ironically.

Behind Mark's simple statement *they crucified him* lie a number of assumptions, commonly understood in Mark's day, about the nature of crucifixion. After bearing the transverse part of his cross to the site, the prisoner was affixed to the upright stake either by ropes or by nailing through the wrists and feet. A seat was provided, not for comfort, but to protract the time of dying. A fiendish refinement of the seat consisted of adding a sharp point, so that the one who sat on it did not get overly comfortable.

Sometimes days were required for crucified persons to die. It is theorized that death was brought on by exposure, utter fatigue, and probably lung collapse leading to suffocation. The person literally choked to death. In any case it was a particularly agonizing way to die, which was indeed its very purpose.

The soldiers' gambling for Jesus' garments (verse 24) is based on the practice of giving the attendants the possessions of the condemned. The scene has also been elaborated with the help especially of Psalm 22. Mark notes that *it was the third hour,* (NIV) when they crucified him (verse 25), or about *9:00 in the morning* (NRSV).

The charge against the condemned person was usually written down and attached to the cross. The note that this charge read *The King of the Jews* (verse 26) indicates the political nature of the charges which led to Jesus' execution.

Jesus is bracketed by *two robbers* (NIV) or *bandits* (NRSV) (verse 27). Since the term translated *robbers* is often used by Josephus to refer to Zealots, or political revolutionaries, it may be the case that these robbers were not ordinary thieves, but insurrectionists against Rome.

The mocking of Jesus at the cross is also based in Scripture (see Psalm 22:7-8, 16-18). The scorners are not named, but presumably are those who sought his execution, since they bring up again the accusation about threatening the *temple* (verse 29; see 14:58). The sarcastic *Save yourself, and come down from the cross!* (verse 30) assumes the implicit claim to divine power for which the charge of blasphemy was lodged.

The earlier named enemies of Jesus, the *chief priests and scribes* (NRSV) or *teachers of the law* (NIV) (verse 31), add their cruel mocking to the enmity towards Jesus. If he is *the Christ, the King of Israel* (verse 32), he should be able to *come down now from the cross*. In effect, the authorities say: Vindicate yourself, and we will believe in you. And even those who were crucified with him also taunted him (verse 32; see, however, the different treatment in Luke 23:40-43).

The scene draws to a conclusion. The darkness *over the whole land* (verse 33) from 12:00 to 3:00 in the afternoon signifies the deed being done. It is reminiscent of Amos 8:9, as indeed the whole story takes place in the context of the fulfillment of the divine purpose as disclosed beforehand in Scripture. *At the ninth hour* (NIV) or *at three o'clock* (NRSV) (verse 34) Jesus cried out, in Aramaic, quoting Psalm 22:1. Mark then gives a Greek translation for the benefit of his readers who do not understand the language.

The bystanders (verse 35) misunderstand Jesus' cry as a call for *Elijah*. The Talmud attests to the belief that Elijah would come to the aid of the distressed. The similarity of sound in the words *Eli* (my God) and *Eli-yah* (Elijah) could account for the confusion.

The identity of the *one* who ran and brought a *sponge with vinegar* (verse 36) for Jesus is not clear. The vinegar would likely be *posca*, a sour wine favored by Roman soldiers, so the one who *put it on a stick and gave it* to him to drink would seem to be a soldier. But it is not likely that a soldier would have understood, much less misunderstood, that Jesus was calling for Elijah. We probably have here two independent traditions relating to Jesus' outcry from the cross which have been fused together.

Mark reports the death of Jesus almost matter-of-factly. Jesus gave a loud cry, *and breathed his last* (verse 37). The cry is like the despairing utterance in verse 34. Jesus does not die a "nice death" in Mark; he goes out in horrifying agony, seemingly with the sense of having been totally left alone by God to his fate in the world.

Portents at the birth and death of great figures are common in ancient literature. Similarly, Mark reports the rending of the Temple curtain *in two* (verse 38). The reference is to that veil which enclosed the Holy of Holies, or innermost part of the Temple, where God symbolically dwelled. Only the high priest had access, on Yom Kippur, or the Day of Atonement, when he acted for all the nation. Mark is saying that now, through the death of Jesus, all have access to God. The Temple cult is at an end, and there is no need of an intercessory priest.

Significantly, the *centurion* (commander of 100 troops), a Gentile and a Roman soldier, is the first to make a confession to Jesus as *Son of God*. That he does so before the cross points to the central significance of the crucifixion in evoking faith.

The Burial of Jesus (15:40-47)

The women who are looking on from afar (verse 40) furnish a transition to the empty tomb story. The names of the women agree only generally with those in the other gospels (see Matthew 28:1; Luke 24:10; John 20:1).

Nevertheless, it is not the women who actually bury the body of Jesus, but *Joseph of Arimathea*, said to be a *respected* (NRSV) or *prominent* (NIV) *member of the council* (verse 43). Because it is evening (verse 42) of the sabbath, burial must occur before sundown. (Whether it is also the day of Preparation is yet more problematic; see above on 14:1).

Nothing is otherwise known of Joseph, nor is there certainty about the location of Arimathea. That Joseph was a member of the Sanhedrin and *also himself waiting for the kingdom of God* lends respectability to the story. Jesus does not die without friends in high places, even though Joseph has to take courage (verse 43) to do his kindly deed. He is a minor model of discipleship: hidden, but at least courageous.

Joseph *bought a linen cloth* (verse 46) in which he wraps the body of Jesus before laying it in a *tomb which had been cut* (NIV) or *hewn* (NRSV) *out of a rock.* Burial in a shroud would have been customary, according to a decree of the rabbi Gamaliel II. The tomb would have been outside Jerusalem, as no burials were allowed within the city.

Joseph's rolling a stone against the door of the tomb further underscores the finality of Jesus' death, and that none could enter easily or leave the tomb. The women who saw where he was laid (verse 47) are those who participate in the empty tomb experience.

The description of the tomb as *hewn* (NRSV) or *cut* (NIV) *out of the rock* (verse 46) accords with the practice of creating burial sites out of lime rock, with bodies placed in either a receptacle hollowed out of the wall, or laid on a ledge around the wall. To prevent grave robbers from entering a heavy stone was set into a track which allowed the stone to roll downward across the opening.

No one really knows where Jesus was buried. There was no practice of mourning at the tomb, as was often customary, for the reason that there was no body there to be mourned. And also for that reason there was no need to preserve a memory of where the tomb was.

§ § § § § § §

The Message of Mark 15

This chapter brings to a climax Mark's story of Jesus' passion. It is a powerful portrayal of the reality of Jesus' condemnation, crucifixion, and death. The question profoundly posed by the Passion narrative is whether one can see in this deeply wounded and humiliated figure the very action of God. That is the challenge of faith.

Let us set forth the following themes in summary.

§ Jesus' appearance before Pilate raises issues of justice. We can say that Jesus was treated unjustly, but to do so is only to make an interesting observation. What is acutely important in Mark is that this one who suffered unjustly did so in order that all the world, including those who commit injustice, might go free.

§ The single most striking thing in Mark's portrayal of the crucifixion is the terrible agony with which Jesus faces his fate and dies. He goes to his death not like, say, Socrates, cheerfully drinking the cup. Jesus' cup was from the start an anguished one. The cost of redemption included a separation in the very being of God.

§ From the death scene of Jesus Mark draws lessons in discipleship. There is no escaping the call to take up the cross, and it may lead to something so humiliating that one can feel severed from God. And no one should count on a miraculous deliverance.

§ The story of Jesus' burial offers a tiny shaft of light in the tunnel of darkness. There were a few—some ordinary women, a compassionate member of the Sanhedrin—who clung to their faithfulness and acted out of devotion. The history of the church is like that. Even in the worst of times God has witnesses.

§ § § § § § §

Introduction to This Chapter

Mark now brings his story to its conclusion. It is a strange conclusion. The women mentioned in 15:40 come to anoint the body of Jesus and find the tomb empty. Inside they encounter a young man, who is obviously an angel. He tells them that Jesus has risen, and to go and relate to the disciples that Jesus will meet them in Galilee. The women say nothing, but flee out of the tomb in fear and astonishment. The Gospel ends in this seemingly unsatisfactory way, with no appearance of Jesus narrated.

Here is an outline of this chapter.
I. The Women at the Tomb (16:1-8)
II. Problems in the Text of Mark (16:9-20)

The Women at the Tomb (16:1-8)

Certain women come after the sabbath to perform the duties of a mortician, which could not have been accomplished on the sabbath. The women named are those in 15:40, though the list is not identical with 15:47. They come to anoint Jesus (verse 1), in keeping with the Jewish custom of putting aromatic spices on the body. The Jews were not familiar with Egyptian embalming practices.

The *first day of the week* (verse 2) was the day after the sabbath, which, as the name implies, was the seventh or last day of the week. The Christian Sunday arose on the basis of the Resurrection and is not the same as the sabbath observance. Sunday is the first day of the week.

The women come very early, soon after sunrise. Their conversation seems strange. They ask, *Who will roll away the stone for us from the entrance of the tomb?* If the women were indeed those who had witnessed the burial, they would surely have known how difficult it would be for them to enter the tomb. Why then did they not come prepared for that problem? This question may point to the fact that the burial and the discovery of the tomb were originally independent traditions.

The women, looking up, discover to their apparent surprise that the stone has already been rolled back (verse 4). The comment that the stone covering the entrance is *very large* indirectly reflects the surprise of the women that the stone has been moved. The young man who is found *sitting on the right side* and *dressed in a white robe* (verse 5) is an angel. The word for angel means *messenger*, and angels were originally thought of as God's emissaries to deliver divine communications.

The *alarm* of the women is a traditional element in stories of encounters with the divine. Also typical is the opening line of the angel, *Do not be alarmed.* Calming the human reactions is a feature of divine encounter stories. What is important is the message of the angel (verse 6).

The women are then instructed to go and tell the disciples and Peter that Jesus is going before them to Galilee, and they will see him there. This statement is highly revealing for Markan theology. The central core is, of course, the proclamation of the Resurrection. Mark provides no description of the resurrected Jesus.

The invitation to the women to see the place where they laid Jesus provides a ground for the women to cling to the Resurrection. It is not a proof, but along with the interpreting word gives hope of the Resurrection. The interesting note in this line is the *they*, which hardly agrees with the story of the burial by Joseph of

Arimathea as his solitary deed. It could be that this *they* reflects an earlier version of the burial of Jesus, in which he was buried not by a kindly Joseph, but by anonymous others as a final act of humiliation. There is a further hint of such a tradition, antedating the present tomb stories, in Acts 13:29. It would, in fact, have been normal to bury crucified persons without relatives to claim the body in a common criminal's grave.

The women are instructed to tell the disciples that the risen one will meet them in Galilee. The instruction recalls the note in 14:28, which seems to anticipate some kind of appearance in Galilee. The specific reference to Peter reflects his priority in the Resurrection appearance tradition (see 1 Corinthians 15:5). The disciples are to be told that they will see him in Galilee.

The women then react in what seems to us to be a strange way. They flee from the tomb in fear (verse 8), and they say nothing to anyone. Mark's language is very strong; the word *amazement* (NRSV) or *bewildered* (NIV) literally suggests that the women were out of their minds. Their fear stifles any reporting of their experience.

When this story is treated as a straightforward historical account, questions arise that simply cannot be answered. Why are the women so afraid? Why do they disobey the angelic instructions? And if they say nothing, how then do the disciples ever find out about the tomb and the meeting in Galilee? We must ask about the message Mark wishes to convey. And even at this level there are peculiarities in the text that are difficult to resolve. For example, if Mark truly ended at verse 8, why does he have a promise of an appearance in Galilee that goes unfulfilled? Some have thought that this problem with the text does require a different ending, and that Mark originally did conclude with some such Galilean appearance. Others think that *Galilee* was for Mark a kind of cipher for the locus of the Parousia, and therefore a follow-up cannot be given because the Parousia has not yet occurred.

There is another possibility, however, as to why Mark ends his work in this rather enigmatic way. Perhaps he did not wish to overplay the value of the empty tomb. After all, the empty tomb does not prove the Resurrection. It remains a sign for faith, but does not replace faith or negate it. Neither is the tomb such a sign that it allows the believer to think he or she can somehow escape the cross. There is no jumping past the cross right into the tomb, for even there does not lie the certainty that can simply override the agony of suffering.

Problems in the Text of Mark (16:9-20)

This chapter has long posed a severe textual problem. A great many manuscripts carry the chapter through verse 16 (the KJV, for example); other old texts conclude at verse 8. Within verses 9-16 there are further additions. The Revised Standard Version and most modern versions follow the strongest manuscript tradition and end Mark at verse 8.

Yet not only is the ending there peculiar from a narrative point of view, it is even grammatically odd. It concludes (in Greek) with a preposition that is almost never at the end of a sentence, much less a book. This grammatical problem is what probably led to the creation of additional endings for Mark.

In verses 9-20 an appearance to Mary Magdalene is reported, followed by appearances to other disciples. The eleven are visited by Jesus and given their commission to preach around the world. In the course of that instruction Jesus recounts the signs which the disciples may expect to accompany their work. These signs include speaking in tongues, casting out demons, handling serpents, and drinking poisonous things without harm.

§ § § § § § §

The Message of Mark 16

The Markan story of the discovery of the empty tomb is remarkably restrained. Already in that restraint is one of its lessons. For Mark does not encourage any sort of "glory" theology based upon the empty tomb. Certainly the proclamation is central: He is risen, he is not here. But such a proclamation must be taken in the context of faith. The good news of the empty tomb is good news only to faith. There remain other ways to interpret an empty tomb besides the idea of Resurrection.

Let us summarize the insights that this chapter conveys to us in the following statements.

§ The questioning and downcast women show that they have not been alive to God's possibilities in Christ. They continued to live in the realm dominated by death. The idea of a resurrection was too overwhelming for them to comprehend. Even after inspecting the tomb they were obviously not convinced.

§ The empty tomb remains a sign for faith. The story of the women at the tomb says that there is hope beyond the cross, even though there is no way past the cross. But only faith can grasp that possibility.

§ Faith does rest upon the evidence posed by the empty tomb. It is certainly likely that Jesus' tomb was empty, but any number of other interpretations could be put upon that fact. The ultimate ground of faith is the encounter with the present and living Lord.

§ § § § § § §

Glossary of Terms

Agape: The Greek for "love" in the sense of an attitude of caring and compassion for the other person without regard to worth or merits. It is not based on emotions, but is an act of the will.

Beelzebul: Means *lord of the flies* and is a derogatory term for Satan. Probably originally came from a word meaning *lord of the house.*

Booths: A festival in Judaism, taking place in the fall, and celebrating the period of wandering in the wilderness when the law was given. A booth was a temporary shelter constructed of limbs and leaves in which the pilgrim dwelled during the time of observance. Also known as Tabernacles.

Centurion: A commander of 100 troops in the Roman army. Centurions usually came up through the ranks.

Cohort: A battalion of 600 troops.

Decapolis: The word means *ten cities,* and refers to the group of ten Greek city-states in the Transjordan area.

Denarius: A Latin word denoting a value of money, often quoted at about eighteen to twenty cents. The denarius was the normal daily wage of an average worker.

Epiphany: From the Greek, meaning *manifestation* or *divine revelation.*

Gethsemane: The garden upon the Mount of Olives where Jesus and some disciples went following the Last Supper. Its location is not precisely known, but various churches are erected on what is presumed to be the site. The name means, in Aramaic, *oil vat*.

Golgotha: The site of Jesus' crucifixion. Its location is unknown. The word means *skull*, but why it was called that is no longer known. Modern conjecture suggests that the land was shaped like a skull.

Hellenistic: Of or pertaining to the age of Greek rule. The Hellenes were Greeks, and the Hellenistic age began with the conquest of the civilized world by Alexander the Great in 333 B.C.

Herod Antipas: One of the sons of Herod the Great. Antipas was given rule over Galilee and Perea at the death of his father, and ruled from 4 B.C. to A.D. 39.

Herodias: Married to Herod Antipas, her hostility towards John the Baptist and his criticism led to John's death. According to Josephus, she was actually married to another half-brother of Antipas, not Philip, while Philip was in fact married to Salome, Herodias' daughter.

Josephus: (first name Flavius); Jewish historian of the first century. Composed many valuable histories of the Jews.

Kingdom of God: Also can be translated as *Rule of God* or *Reign of God*. It does not refer to a territory, but to God's dynamic rule as king. By Jesus' day the idea of the Kingdom had taken on apocalyptic or at least eschatological associations in many quarters.

Legion: The basic unit in the Roman army, consisting of 6,000 men.

Lepta: Plural of *lepton*, the smallest coin. It is estimated at one fourth of a sixteenth of a denarius, about what a workman might expect to earn in a day.

Messiah, messianic: The word means *anointed one*, and refers to that David-like figure expected to come and exercise justice and to rule on behalf of God.

Mishnah: A collection of oral laws compiled in the second century A.D. It is an extensive summation of the interpretation of the Torah or law of Moses as made over several centuries by the scribes or experts in the law.

Mount of Olives: Sometimes also called *Olivet* (see Luke 19:29). Part of a mountain range east of Jerusalem, connected with the growing of olive groves.

Nero: Full name Nero Claudius Caesar, mad emperor of Rome in the mid-sixties. After persecuting Christians he finally died by his own hand.

Nisan: The first month of the Hebrew calendar, from approximately March 15 to April 15. The Hebrew calendar was lunar.

Parousia: Greek word used in the New Testament to refer to Jesus' coming at the end of time. The New Testament does not speak of Jesus' *second coming.*

Passover: Derived from the passing-over of the destroying angel at the Exodus from Egypt. The word refers to the event and the first of the three pilgrim feasts celebrated during the liturgical year.

Pax Romana: Latin meaning *Peace of Rome.* It described the Roman policy of guaranteeing peace within the borders of the empire. Political rebellion was not tolerated.

Pharisees: The Pharisees were a lay movement, mostly open to new ideas, and especially characterized by dedication to observance of all the law. They probably came into being in the second century B.C.

Philip: Son of Herod the Great, half-brother of Herod Antipas, married to Salome, according to Josephus. He ruled a number of territories after his father's death, from approximately 4 B.C. to A.D. 34.

Phoenicia: Originally a territory of an ancient seagoing, trading people. In Jesus' day Phoenicia was no longer a nation, but the term was used geographically to refer to certain cities in Syria (Tyre, Sidon).

Procurators: The procurators or governors ruled over Judea after Archaelaus, son of Herod the great, was deposed for incompetence.

Quadrans: Latin for an amount of money, very small, about one sixty-fourth of a denarius.

GLOSSARY OF TERMS

Sadducees: A priestly group, generally associated with the aristocracy, rather conservative politically and theologically, and had their center of power in the Sanhedrin and the Temple. They disappeared after the war with Rome was effectively settled in A.D. 70.

Sanhedrin: The highest legal body in Judaism. It ruled on matters of law and tried significant cases. Whether it possessed the power of capital punishment at the time of Jesus is still debated.

Synagogue: From the Greek, meaning to *gather together*, or *bring together*. The synagogue likely originated in the time of the Exile and became one of Judaism's most enduring institutions. It was a place for corporate worship, for instruction in and study of the law.

Tabernacles: See *Booths*.

Talmud: The book of oral tradition gathered over several centuries. The *Mishnah* is part of the Talmud, which was not codified until about the fifth century A.D.

Torah: Hebrew term referring to the law. Its apparent meaning is *instruction*, or *guidance*.

Unleavened Bread: The feast that inaugurated Passover observance, also the name of the bread which was eaten in connection with that celebration. Leaven is yeast. The significance of the yeastless bread is to symbolize the haste of departure from Egypt.

Yahweh: The divine name for God in the Old Testament. Originally thought to be *Jehovah*, the correct pronunciation is now seen to be Yahweh. The pronunciation was lost because the name was considered to be too sacred to be spoken.

Yom Kippur: The Day of Atonement, in the month of Tishri or the seventh month, when the high priest entered the Holy of Holies, where the throne of God was, and made atonement for the whole nation. It was a great day of celebration in Judaism.

Guide to Pronunciation

Ahimelech: Ah-HIH-muh-lek
Bartimaeus: Bar-tih-MAY-us
Beelzebul: Bee-ELL-zeh-bull
Bethphage: BETH-fah-jee
Bethsaida: Beth-SAY-duh
Capernaum: Kah-PER-nah-um
Cyrene: Sigh-REE-nee
Dalmanutha: Dal-mah-NOO-thah
Ephphatha: EFF-fah-thah
Gehenna: Geh-HEH-nuh
Gennesaret: Geh-NESS-ah-ret
Gerasa: GEH-rah-sah
Gerasene: GER-ah-seen
Gedara: GEH-dah-rah
Gergesa: GER-geh-sah
Herodias: Heh-ROH-dee-us
Kephas: KAY-fass
Nisan: NIGH-san
Parousia: Par-oo-SEE-uh
Philistine: FIL-iss-teen
Phoenicia: Foh-NEE-shuh
Salome: Sal-OH-may
Shema: Sheh-MAH
Sicarius: Sih-CAHR-ree-us
Yom Kippur: YOME-Kih-POOR
Zebedee: ZEH-buh-dee

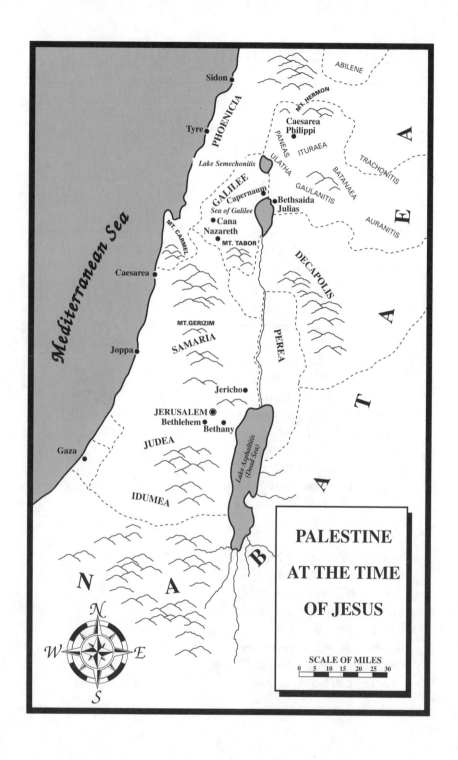

PALESTINE

AT THE TIME

OF JESUS

SCALE OF MILES

0 5 10 15 20 25 30